MW01283067

To:

_____

From:

_____

Date:

_____

Visit Christian Art Gifts, Inc., at www.christianartgifts.com.

Beautifully Blended: 101 Devotions to Encourage Couples in Blended Families

Previously published by Worthy Inspired under the title *Stepparenting with Grace: A Devotional for Blended Families*. Copyright © 2018. Revised and updated.

© 2025 by Gayla Grace. All rights reserved.

Published by Christian Art Gifts, Inc., Bloomingdale, IL, USA.

First edition 2025.

Designed by Christian Art Gifts, Inc.

Cover and interior images used under license from Shutterstock.com.

Most Christian Art titles may be purchased at bulk discounts by churches, nonprofits, and corporations. For more information, please email SpecialMarkets@cagifts.com.

ISBN 978-1-63952-902-5

Printed in China.

30 29 28 27 26 25
10 9 8 7 6 5 4 3 2 1

Beautifully
BLENDED

101 Devotions to Encourage
Couples in Blended Families

GAYLA GRACE

Christian Art
PUBLISHERS

"Compact doses of grace for your blended family. That's what this book is. But though these devotionals may be easily consumed, they are dense, packed with practical wisdom that will point you in the right direction. Gayla Grace is a leading voice in the care of blended families and an expert in stepfamily relationships. Combined with her life experience of over 27 years as a mom, stepmom, and wife qualifies this resource as "one-of-a-kind." I trust her voice, and so should you."

—Ron Deal, Director of FamilyLife Blended, stepfamily therapist, speaker, and author of over fifteen resources including the bestselling *Building Love Together in Blended Families* (with Gary Chapman) and *The Smart Stepfamily*.

"Beautifully Blended offers valuable insight into the unique dynamics of stepfamily life and heartfelt solutions to common struggles. Packed with 'been there, understand that' guidance, Gayla Grace has lived in the trenches and offers biblically based help in every devotional. If you want to thrive in your blended family relationships, read this book."

—Dave and Ann Wilson, hosts of the *FamilyLife Today* podcast and authors of *Vertical Marriage*.

"Gayla Grace supplies exactly what's needed to encourage and inspire stepfamilies in her devotional, *Beautifully Blended*. Gayla understands what works and what doesn't work in stepfamilies, both from her own experience and from counseling others. With a highly readable and relatable style, Gayla writes in a 'come alongside' manner with invaluable advice, much like talking to a wise and trusted friend who has walked in your shoes."

—Carol Boley, coauthor of *But I'm NOT a Wicked Stepmother! Secrets of Successful Blended Families*

"*Beautifully Blended* is a must read. Gayla Grace shares her personal anecdotes while providing stepfamily advice that really works. Each devotion is designed to strengthen your faith and renew your resolve. It's realistic, comforting, and inspiring. This book will change the way you look at stepfamily life."

—Brenda Ockun, founder and publisher of
StepMom Magazine

"If you've said yes to stepparenting, this devotional is for you. Gayla Grace has written over a hundred readings that address every concern, obstacle, and fear you face. With powerful Scripture, encouraging nuggets of truth for each day, personal stories, and poignant applications, this book will give you answers to your questions, strength for your soul, and grace for the everyday challenges of life. It also makes a great gift for anyone who is a stepparent."

—Carol Kent, speaker and author of *He Holds My Hand: Experiencing God's Presence & Protection*

To my husband and fellow stepparent, Randy,
who never wavers in his unconditional love
and support for me and our blended family.

To our children, Adrianne, Payton, Jamie, Jodi, and Nathan,
who fill my days with joy and meaning and
have taught me how to love and be loved.

To blended family couples everywhere
who need encouragement and inspiration.
You can do this! God calls special
people to do His hardest work.

*Don't copy the behavior and customs of this world, but let God
transform you into a new person by changing the way you think.*

Romans 12:2 NLT

Contents

Perseverance Counts

Seek Wisdom

Blended Family Blessings

The Beauty of Grace

Coping with Grief

The Power of Fun and Laughter

Building Relationships That Go the Distance

God's Redeeming Power

Introduction

As a young stepmom, I longed for a devotional that offered encouraging words for my unique needs and help for marriage in a blended family. Lonely, discouraged, and fearful, I tried to navigate the journey. I found limited resources to help combat my emotions during a confusing season.

Almost three decades later, there is still a lack of devotionals that focus on the needs of blended families—the dynamics are complicated, the demands are many. Every day, stepfamily couples experience challenges they can't control. How do you form a united team in parenting? Who do you talk to about expectations that haven't come to pass? How do you manage your frustration over constant schedule changes from a former spouse? When will you get time alone with your spouse? Or your own kids? How do you cope with rejection in your own home or combat the loss of identity you feel?

It's hard. I understand. But God walks with us.

Through this devotional, I pray you'll find contentment in thorny circumstances, peace in disharmony, and clarity in confusion. My aim is to move you to a daily pursuit of grace.

God's grace offers new beginnings. I've seen it work in my own life. After my divorce, I experienced a dark season of failure and defeat. I was raised in a Christian home with parents who were married for sixty-five years; divorce was never an option for them. How could *I* go down that road? Yet I did.

I didn't believe I deserved another chance at marriage. With two young daughters to raise, I wasn't looking for a husband. But God demonstrated His love and mercy for me. He brought someone into my life whose last name was Grace, and now I carry that name every day as a reminder. *Thank You, Jesus.*

Grace offers second chances. In marriage. In blended family relationships. Even against the backdrop of failure. But we must first accept God's grace in our own lives. Then, we can offer it to others.

I pray that through these devotions, you'll find the courage to seek grace, the confidence to push past your fears, and a craving for God and His Word to find comfort and clarity on your journey.

Gayla Grace
May 2024

TRUST GOD

Trusting God

"For my thoughts are not your thoughts, neither are your ways my ways,"
declares the LORD. "As the heavens are higher than the earth, so are my
ways higher than your ways and my thoughts than your thoughts."

ISAIAH 55:8–9

One phone call is all it took to change our stepfamily forever. "I just got the news. She passed away earlier today," my husband, Randy, said. After a yearlong struggle with cancer, the beloved mom of my teenage stepchildren had passed. My stepchildren would now face life without her. The finality of Randy's words sent chills down my spine. My heart ached for them.

Randy and I had been praying for healing for his former wife. But that didn't happen. I knew the effects of the loss would soon be felt in our home. We had weathered some rough storms in our nine years as a stepfamily and were finally settling into comfortable relationships. I was thankful for our newfound harmony. Losing their mom would leave a cavernous hole in my stepchildren's hearts. It was only natural that our relationships might suffer.

The path before us lay unmapped. My mind was bombarded with questions that had no answers.

- Would the children move across state lines and come live with us?
- Could our home accommodate two more?
- How would they cope as they struggled to accept their mom was gone?
- What could we do to help with their troubled emotions?

I had to trust God.
Solutions didn't surface quickly. We waded through months of confusion and

anxiety. At times, Randy and I didn't see eye to eye. Tension mounted. Tempers flared. My faith wavered as we faced trying circumstances I couldn't change.

Finally, I let go. I surrendered to God's plan, and I trusted His guiding hand.

My stepdaughter opted to continue college and didn't relocate. My stepson lived with his sister, younger half-brother, and stepdad for almost a year before finally moving in with us. During that time, we encountered uncertainty and questions. Peace came only as we gave up the need for control, trusting God with the outcome.

It's been almost two decades now since my stepchildren lost their mom. They endured a difficult season, but they found healing for their loss. They're both thriving as adults, and I'm thankful for healthy, loving relationships with them.

I still struggle with trusting God at times. It's difficult for me to let go. Too often, I want it to be *my* way, not His way. But I've learned He can be trusted, even when I don't understand. I know His ways are sovereign.

Help me, heavenly Father, to trust Your ways,
even when I don't understand. Guide me through
our tumultuous waters to sunnier days ahead.

THOUGHT FOR THE DAY

We can trust God, even when
we don't understand His plan.

El Shaddai: God Almighty

The LORD will fight for you; you need only to be still.

EXODUS 14:14

"We cannot change the cards we are dealt, just how we play the hand." Professor Randy Pausch spoke those words in "The Last Lecture," a talk he gave at Carnegie Mellon University. He had just learned his pancreatic cancer, diagnosed a year prior, was terminal. Pausch didn't ask for pity or talk about his challenges. Instead, he encouraged those in the audience to work toward their dreams, overcome their obstacles, and seize every moment. Although he'd been dealt a difficult hand, he chose to focus only on a positive perspective.

Blended family life includes its own set of difficulties. Maybe the hand you've been dealt includes a defiant stepchild. Or a manipulative ex-spouse. Or a loneliness you can't shake because no one understands the stepparent journey you walk.

God's promises give us hope. And El Shaddai, God Almighty, is capable of fulfilling His promises. The story of Abraham confirms His all-sufficiency. Genesis 17:1–2 says, "I am God Almighty; walk before me faithfully and be blameless. Then I will make my covenant between me and you and will greatly increase your numbers." Although Abraham and Sarah were well past childbearing age, God brought them a son, Isaac. God later fulfilled His promise to make Abraham's descendants "as numerous as the stars in the sky and as the sand on the seashore" (Genesis 22:17).

If we dig deeper into his life, we find a stepfamily problem around Abraham's sons, Isaac and Ishmael (Genesis 21). Abraham's first son, Ishmael, was born to his slave Hagar because Sarah had become impatient waiting on God to give her a child and offered Hagar to her husband. When Ishmael's half-brother, Isaac, was born, Sarah mistreated Hagar. We find great strife between the two women, and Sarah tells Abraham to send Hagar and Ishmael away.

Abraham is naturally distressed. God tells him to listen to Sarah, and He will take care of his son. The next morning, Abraham gives Hagar food and water and sends her and Ishmael off to wander in the desert. What a painful departure that must have been! But we see God's provision: "God was with the boy as he grew up" (Genesis 21:20). Later, Scripture tells us Ishmael lived 137 years and was the father of twelve tribal leaders, as God had promised.

Modern stepfamily issues include strife and separation as well, but we can be assured God will provide for our needs. We can trust the all-sufficiency of El Shaddai, God Almighty.

Thank You, Father, for Your promises. When my faith wavers, remind me that You are God Almighty.

THOUGHT FOR THE DAY

When we trust El Shaddai to fulfill His promises, we find hope for every need.

Expect the Unexpected

I lift up my eyes to the mountains—where does my help come from?
My help comes from the Lord, the Maker of heaven and earth. He will
not let your foot slip—he who watches over you will not slumber.

PSALM 121:1–3

When the unexpected happens, we need a reminder to lift up our eyes and find help from the Lord. It's a simple command. Look up and find hope. What are you facing today? Have you experienced an unexpected detour? It happens in blended families. Often. Custody battles. Children changing residences. Sudden illness or even death. Job loss. Addiction. Child support changes. Miscarriage.

How do you cope? In his book *Eyes Up*, Pastor Louie Giglio says we must move from "self-dependency to God-ability." We often start with self-dependency, don't we? But God-ability offers so much more.

My stepmom friend Nicole desperately wanted a child of her own. She loves her stepchildren, but they have an active mom in their lives, which naturally limits her maternal role. She and her husband prayed about the decision to have a mutual child and felt comfortable moving forward.

When Nicole became pregnant, she had no idea of the bumpy road ahead. Her first pregnancy ended in miscarriage. She and her husband were sad, naturally, but knew they could try again. She miscarried again. And again. And again. Finally, she began to see other doctors. She and her husband prayed about their next steps, but they never sensed they should quit trying. As Psalm 121 suggests, they looked up for help.

Nicole commented about the twists and turns they walked: "This journey has been nothing short of grace and mercy and redemption. God never said it would be easy, but He always promises it will be worthwhile. I've drawn the closest I ever have been to God in this journey of loss and infertility over the last three years, and I would do it again just to have my Jesus moments! Abba Papa is a great daddy!"

Nicole lost eight babies—yes, eight!—before she finally conceived and birthed her son, Caleb, who will forever be their miracle child. "God always had us, and those babies, in the palm of His hand," she said. "God is always faithful."

I don't know what detours you will encounter on your stepfamily pilgrimage, but you can expect one, two, or even eight. When you need answers to your questions, change the direction of your eyes. Look up!

Thank You, heavenly Father, for reassuring me that I can look up and find help when I need it. I don't have to walk alone.

THOUGHT FOR THE DAY

We find answers to the unexpected detours of blended family life when we look up.

Trusting God's Promises

Trust in the Lord with all your heart and lean not on your own understanding; in all your ways submit to him, and he will make your paths straight.

PROVERBS 3:5–6

God has the answer—whatever you face. Do you struggle with a mentally unstable child? A spouse who doesn't support your role as a stepparent? Maybe you can't get past the outsider feeling in your home. When suffering prevails, we're quick to call a friend, meet a stepparent for lunch, or even consult with a pastor regarding our struggle. Those people might have an opinion to consider, but that should never be the ultimate decision-maker for us. "For the foolishness of God is wiser than human wisdom, and the weakness of God is stronger than human strength" (1 Corinthians 1:25). Do we believe Paul's words?

Perhaps we don't trust God. Life feels unfair. God didn't answer our prayer the way we wanted. We still have disharmony in our home. We've failed at bonding with our stepchild. A custody battle looms without answers. It's easy to blame God.

As Christians, we quote the familiar verse, Romans 8:28, when we don't understand our struggles: "We know that in all things God works for the good of those who love Him, who have been called according to His purpose." But in the midst of suffering, that can feel like a kick to the gut. What we're going through doesn't feel good. Can we really trust that God has a purpose in it?

Yes, absolutely! Sometimes, the things God uses for good in our lives aren't good in themselves, though. He doesn't ask us to deny the reality of sickness, hardship, sin, and other evils. Grief is not joy. Betrayal is not faithfulness. Heartache is not peace. But we can trust God to bring good out of evil. God uses our suffering for lasting good—the greatest of which is conformity to the character of the Lord Jesus Christ that happens when we trust and surrender to Him.

Paul says, "*We know ...* God works for the good." He doesn't say, "We *feel* God is working for our good," or "We *see* God is working for our good." We might feel discouraged or defeated. Perhaps we see destruction or mental illness. The key is to let knowledge override feelings. We can trust His character. He sacrificed His only Son to save us from our sins. He will work to bring good to those who love Him.

Thank You for Your promise, Lord, that good will prevail,
regardless of my circumstances. I trust You. Comfort me when I'm sad.

THOUGHT FOR THE DAY

You can trust God to bring good from your suffering.

Painful Transitions

Those who are dominated by the sinful nature think about
sinful things, but those who are controlled by the Holy
Spirit think about things that please the Spirit.

ROMANS 8:5 NLT

I could hear the heartache behind the words as the stepdad of three told his story. After an extended absence from their lives, the biological father of his stepchildren surfaced and asked for a relationship with his teenage children. The stepdad had played a significant role in the children's lives but was suddenly pushed aside into a dispensable position. His tears told the story of a hurt he couldn't change.

Blended families experience transitions that traditional families don't. A stepchild's change of residence or upheaval in the other home from divorce, remarriage, relocation, or a new baby creates transition, often uninvited and unwanted. The climate in your home changes when noncustodial parents fluctuate the amount of time and energy they dedicate to their children. Without renewed effort toward harmony, relationships easily become embittered.

In our own family, my ex-husband reentered the picture after years of alcoholism and homelessness. I reacted angrily to his desire for a place in our children's lives. Randy had loved and provided for my girls during my ex-husband's absence, and he didn't deserve to be pushed away.

After years of trying to control their relationships, I finally surrendered. I recognized that my girls needed to know more about their biological father. I agreed to a visitation arrangement with the man who had previously abandoned them, acknowledging that it was part of God's plan. Thankfully, I watched a beautiful relationship with Randy and his stepdaughters continue to thrive.

If we seek to control circumstances we can't change (such as relationship building we don't like), we'll find frustration and anxiety. If we choose to surrender and trust God with the outcome, we'll find peace.

It takes courage to surrender to an unexpected and unwanted transition. But with God's help, we can find peace, even during unsettling circumstances. The apostle Paul, writing from prison, said, "I have learned the secret of being content in any and every situation, whether well fed or hungry, whether living in plenty or in want. I can do all this through Him who gives me strength" (Philippians 4:12–13).

Only when Christ's strength guides our surrendered steps can we endure the pain and uncertainty that accompany unwanted transition.

Heavenly Father, transition is hard. Help me give up my desire for control and surrender to Your plan. Thank You that I can trust Your ways to be better than mine.

THOUGHT FOR THE DAY

When we choose to surrender instead of seeking to control, we find contentment during transition.

Seek Him First

Look at the birds of the air; they do not sow or reap or
store away in barns, and yet your heavenly Father feeds
them. Are you not much more valuable than they?

MATTHEW 6:26

I stared at the numbers on the paper in disbelief. With my daughter's wedding on the horizon—the first of our five children to walk to the altar—I had made a trip out of state to help with plans.

Visions of flower arrangements, color themes, and catering ideas swirled in my head as we prepared to meet with the wedding coordinator. I wasn't prepared to see the estimated cost of the celebration.

All day long, I thought about those numbers. I considered where we could cut costs to make it work. I sent a text to a friend who had offered to sell her wedding décor at a reduced price. Before I went to bed, I prayed that God would provide, fully aware we didn't have enough money set aside for the estimated cost.

I woke to a text from my friend. "I donated that décor to the church. You can use any of it for free. Contact the event coordinator for help." *Thank You, Jesus.* God had responded to my plea with a few expenses covered.

When I returned home, I continued to pray that God would provide. The upcoming months included a frenzy of wedding activities. Then, one evening, my husband came in from work and, with a smile on his face, handed me a folded letter. I opened it and began to cry. The company he worked for had recently sold to a new owner. In honor of the hard work of those who had contributed to the profit from years past, they were awarded bonuses. Randy had received a check in the exact amount we needed to cover the unaccounted-for wedding expenses. What a blessing! *Thank You, Jesus.*

Life in a blended family includes unaccounted-for expenses often. We can't control the ebb and flow of child support changes, extracurricular costs we thought the other home would cover, unexpected medical bills, and a host of other expenses that often pop up. But we can trust that God knows what we need, and He will provide. "Seek first His kingdom and His righteousness, and all these things will be given to you as well" (Matthew 6:33).

Heavenly Father, I often fret about the unending expenses that accompany our large family. Thank You for promising to provide for our needs. Help me to trust You more and worry less.

─── THOUGHT FOR THE DAY ───

We can always trust God to provide for our needs.

Choosing Trust over Fear

Have I not commanded you? Be strong and courageous.
Do not be afraid; do not be discouraged, for the
LORD your God will be with you wherever you go.

JOSHUA 1:9

"Why are you so untrusting, Mom?" my son, Nathan, said with his brow furrowed. "I'm not worried about it." He had let a friend borrow his favorite shin guards, a much-needed soccer item, and wasn't worried his friend might not bring them to the game that night.

His words stung. Why *was* I so untrusting? I folded my arms across my chest as I thought about it.

I knew why. I had recently been hurt by a dear friend and refused to let her back into my heart. Paralyzed by fear, I didn't know how to move forward in that relationship. I suddenly realized the effects.

Later that day, I sat quietly and asked God for an answer to my fear. The story of Joshua and Caleb in Numbers 13–14 came to mind. These two men, along with ten other Israelite leaders, were sent to explore the land of Canaan. For forty days, they wandered, examining the fruit, the towns, and the people who lived there. When they returned, they gave reports of a land that flowed with milk and honey. But some of the spies also spread fear, speaking of large and powerful people living there.

The Israelites questioned whether they should move into this land. They allowed fear to influence them. But Caleb responded, "Do not be afraid of the people of the land, because we will devour them. Their protection is gone, but the LORD is with us. Do not be afraid of them" (Numbers 14:9).

Caleb trusted the Lord more than he feared the people of Canaan. He made a choice that ultimately awarded him the promised land—a gift others didn't get.

But even more than that, Caleb received words of praise from the Lord: "Because my servant Caleb has a different spirit and follows me wholeheartedly, I will bring him into the land he went to, and his descendants will inherit it" (Numbers 14:24).

Did you catch that? Caleb had a "different spirit." I wonder what that means. Perhaps that's a person who forgives when deeply wounded. One who moves past fear and opens her heart again. One who trusts others at their word (like Nathan and his friend, who *did* bring his shin guards back).

I want to live with a different spirit, but at times, I act like one of the ten spies. I allow fear to drive my behavior. I've been wounded in my blended family, and I close my heart. Instead of trusting God's ways, I determine my own way. I listen to others instead of listening to God.

But that sends me back to the wilderness! I want to live in the promised land as one who follows the Lord wholeheartedly—one who chooses trust over fear.

Dear Lord, I want to live like Caleb. But I need Your help. Give me the courage to trust Your ways with every step and follow You to new heights.

┌─────────── THOUGHT FOR THE DAY ───────────┐

When we trust the Lord and His
guiding hand, our fears subside.

└───┘

When Contentment Feels Out of Reach

*And my God will meet all your needs according
to the riches of his glory in Christ Jesus.*

PHILIPPIANS 4:19

Our first grandchild, Harvest Joy, was born in a foreign country, more than 8,000 miles from where we live. Years prior, I had accepted that my daughter and son-in-law were called to serve overseas. I missed them terribly, but I could text, FaceTime, or call to catch up. Having my first grandbaby so far from home carried a different level of sadness.

I'll never forget my first visit when I got to meet Harvest. For two weeks, I held her, rocked her, fed her, sang to her, cuddled with her, and did ALL the things grandmas do. Bliss surrounded me. But then I had to leave. That morning, I cried every time I held Harvest. My whole body ached with sadness as I said goodbye. I was numb as I climbed onto the airplane.

In the beginning, I whined about it—a lot—to anyone who would listen. It felt so unfair. All my friends had grandchildren who lived just down the road or maybe a city over. Why, God?

We are now expecting our second grandchild in a few short weeks. I can't wait for Millie June's arrival—another adorable baby girl, but this time, it's different. She will live in the same town we do!

I've thought a lot about Millie's arrival. I can go to the hospital when my daughter is in labor. I will know exactly when the baby is born. I can experience all the firsts I didn't get to with Harvest. Why couldn't God have provided that before? He must have known that's what I wanted.

I remind myself that God's ways are not my ways; His thoughts are not my thoughts (Isaiah 55:8). I have questions that go unanswered. Why didn't He heal my stepchildren's mother when she was dying of cancer? Why did my husband lose his job? Why does Harvest have to live in a foreign country?

If I truly believe that God's ways are higher than my ways, then I have to believe His ways are best. Even when I don't like His ways or understand His ways.

The question then becomes: Will I still trust Him even if it looks different than what I want? Will I seek contentment amidst heartache, knowing it's God's plan?

I wonder if it makes God sad to watch me grumble about my circumstances, to grumble about *His ways*. I will never find contentment while grumbling.

I can choose to be thankful for a healthy, happy granddaughter even if she lives in a foreign country. I can accept that my stepfamily relationships aren't where I want them to be. I can ask for God's help when I'm discouraged. And in the midst of heartache, I can believe and trust that God will work out all things for His good, in His time.

God is more concerned about our character, our holiness, and our heart than He is about our comfort. He puts us in uncomfortable places to grow us, sanctify us, and prepare us for how He wants to use us. His ways are higher. His ways are best.

*Precious Lord, help me to accept Your ways, even
when I don't understand them. I trust You and
need your help finding contentment today.*

THOUGHT FOR THE DAY

God is more concerned about our character, our
holiness, and our heart, than He is about our comfort.

When a Child Changes Residence

Don't worry about anything; instead, pray about everything.
Tell God what you need, and thank him for all he has done. Then you will
experience God's peace, which exceeds anything we can understand.
His peace will guard your hearts and minds as you live in Christ Jesus.
PHILIPPIANS 4:6–7 NLT

"I want to come live with you, Dad." The stepmom overheard the conversation between her husband and his son. "I've already talked to Mom about it. I want to spend more time with you." *Oh boy,* the stepmom thought.

It's not uncommon for children who have two biological parents involved in their lives to change residence at some point, often during their teenage years. For a nonresidential parent who has longed to have their child live with them, the transition seems exciting. The stepparent, however, often feels apprehensive. Living full-time with stepchildren is quite different than a visit every other weekend.

In another situation, stepchildren who reside in our home might decide to move in with their other parent. When that kind of change occurs, we question and agonize over the decision, particularly as a stepparent. What did I do wrong? Why do they want to leave our home?

It's common for children in blended family homes to change residence at some point, either temporarily or long-term. It might have nothing to do with the dynamics of the residential home, but everything to do with relationship building in the other home. It's important to step back, spend time in prayer, and discuss the decision objectively, trusting God with the outcome.

My stepdaughter moved in with her mom and stepdad, 150 miles away, as an adolescent. I clearly remember the sadness I felt as I set the dinner table every night with one less plate. Although I knew she longed for more time with her mom, I felt like we'd failed her. A few years later, my stepson joined his sister at his mom's house. The sadness and uneasiness appeared again as we questioned and adjusted to the change.

We trusted a sovereign God in the midst of our change. Not long after my stepson moved, his mother was diagnosed with cancer. I was thankful for the time my stepchildren had with her before she passed away. Romans 8:28 resonates with us: "We know that in all things God works for the good of those who love Him, who have been called according to His purpose."

Consider this paradox: Christ's death on the cross looked like failure to many. We know, however, His story ends with a victorious "Amen!" Trust Him.

Thank You, dear Lord, that I can trust Your ways. Calm my heart when we face change in our home. Remind me of Your promise to walk with me when I'm afraid.

THOUGHT FOR THE DAY

We can trust God when change occurs in our home.

The God in Whom I Trust

Therefore do not worry about tomorrow, for tomorrow will
worry about itself. Each day has enough trouble of its own.

MATTHEW 6:34

"My adult stepdaughter's presence brings fear and anxiety," Becky said with her hand trembling. "I don't know what I've done to create such animosity from Nicole, but I don't want to be around her. I don't know how I'm going to get through her birthday celebration."

Becky had married Nicole's dad after a short engagement. Nicole's mom had passed away unexpectedly, and Nicole wasn't ready to have a stepmom in her life. Her wounded soul spilled over to Becky.

Becky's feelings were normal. But her husband didn't want to alienate his daughter and insisted Becky find a way to accommodate, setting Becky up for uncomfortable interactions. "What would you do?" she asked me.

I sat quietly for a moment before I answered. "I would start with prayer," I said. "Your husband obviously wants you and Nicole to have a relationship. Ask God to soften Nicole's heart toward you. I've seen God heal many blended family relationships, but you'll need to be patient. Be prepared to give it time."

I went on to tell Becky about an acrostic our pastor shared recently on what it means to trust God with our difficulties.

T – Take it to the Lord
R – Recognize the greatness of God
U – Unload the problem to God and leave it there
S – Simply ask for God's help
T – Trust God to walk with you, whatever you face

God knows what we need before we ask. In Philippians 4:6–7, the apostle Paul writes, "Do not be anxious about anything, but in every situation, by prayer and petition, with thanksgiving, present your requests to God. And the peace of God, which transcends all understanding, will guard your hearts and your minds in Christ Jesus."

Prayer is our best defense when we encounter relationship issues in our blended family. We can't control how another person responds to us, but we can control how we react. When we pray for someone, we are more likely to react in love and grace. And prayer will bring us peace.

I gave Becky a hug and said, "God isn't asking you to figure it out. He is asking you to *trust* that He already has. Unload the problem to God and leave it there."

Dear Lord, I can't always solve my blended family struggles.
But You can. Intervene on my behalf. Soften the hearts of those who
are hurting. I trust You to walk with me and fill my heart with peace.

THOUGHT FOR THE DAY

Prayer declares our need and discloses our trust in God.

Trust God: Reflect on It

1. When life feels unfair in your blended family, how do you react? Do you trust that "God's ways are higher" (Isaiah 55:9) and wait for His guidance, or do you charge ahead with your own ways?

2. The narrative of Joshua and Caleb, as recounted in Numbers 13–14, serves as a poignant testament to the power of trust in God, even in the face of adversity. Study their story and reflect on how you can apply their lessons in your own life.

3. Where do you struggle with contentment? Will you count your blessings instead of grumbling about circumstances?

4. Do you believe the promise of Exodus 14:14, "The Lord will fight for you?" Where can you apply that to your family?

5. Have you experienced an unwanted change in your home—perhaps a child changing residence? Can you consider the paradox of how change can have positive impacts on your family in the long run? Trust God as you move through difficult emotions.

THE IMPORTANT ROLE
OF A STEPPARENT

The Calling of a Stepparent

Now may the God of peace ... equip you with all you need
for doing his will. May he produce in you, through the power
of Jesus Christ, every good thing that is pleasing to him.

HEBREWS 13:20–21 NLT

"I feel lost. I used to be confident and joyful. Most days now, I feel tired and ambivalent. I don't even know who I am anymore. Can you help?"

My heart ached as I read the stepmom's plea for help. I understood her feelings. It's not unusual to feel lost, uncertain, and confused in our stepparenting role. But we don't have to stay stuck there.

I didn't walk into adulthood with aspirations to be a stepparent. I doubt you did, either. Parenthood is meant to happen within the framework of a single marriage, where a child's own father and mother work together to provide a loving, secure environment. But that doesn't always happen. My husband, Randy, and I raised five kids together in a stepfamily. Now, with only our mutual child left at home, we are in a quieter season of parenting. I often look back to our early years together and consider the differences between blended family and traditional family life. There's really no comparison. The dynamics of a traditional family don't even come close to the complications that stepfamilies face.

That doesn't mean we can't enjoy loving and meaningful relationships in stepfamilies or find joy in our stepparent calling. But we have to work harder, relying on God's help to achieve that. It's not going to happen naturally.

When we accept the calling, we can then find joy in it. Maybe you wanted a child of your own, but God said no. Maybe you started marriage in a traditional family but lost your spouse unexpectedly. The stepparenting role that remarriage has created for you is unplanned and disorienting. Perhaps you struggle raising stepchildren alongside your own children following a divorce. Will you accept the calling God has given you to be a loving, Christlike influence to children you didn't birth?

Well-known pastor and author Andy Stanley says, "Your greatest contribution to the kingdom of God may not be something you do, but someone you raise." If you've been placed in a stepchild's life, God has you there for an important purpose.

When feelings of uncertainty or inadequacy arise, take time to look at yourself through God's eyes. God saw Abram as "the father of many nations" at ninety-nine years old with only one son (Genesis 17:4). God saw Mary as the mother of the Savior when she was yet a girl. God sees you as a capable, loving parent who can make a difference in your stepchild's life like no one else can. I pray you'll embrace the important calling you've been given as a stepparent.

Dear Lord, I struggle with my calling at times.
Give me a fresh perspective that includes a spirit of
thanksgiving for the stepchildren You've entrusted to me.

THOUGHT FOR THE DAY

As stepparents, we're called to play an important role.

Humility Encourages Harmony

When pride comes, then comes disgrace,
but with humility comes wisdom.

PROVERBS 11:2

I didn't want to hear what my husband had to say. We'd been married less than a year, but he'd already noticed patterns with my young daughter, Jamie, that concerned him. Deceiving myself, I believed her unhealthy tendencies would work their way out without intervention. I was wrong.

Jamie's first-grade teacher asked for a conference. I listened with a heavy heart as she described Jamie's nervous ticks in the classroom, her inability to focus, and her general restlessness. I remembered Randy's words. Maybe he was right. Did Jamie need professional help?

As stepparents, we carry an objective view of our stepchildren. It's harder for biological parents to grasp the complete picture of their child, particularly if they're emotionally entangled. How stepparents present their views, however, determines how well they're received. Pride will prevent understanding if we insist our opinion matters more than another's.

Randy described Jamie's behavior with love and compassion, giving specifics of behavior that seemed out of place. I was easily defensive, however, to suggestions that Jamie needed outside help. Pride closed my ears. Didn't I know my own daughter better than he did?

Distrust in the stepparent's opinion can cloud a parent's judgment, particularly in the early years. It helps to tread lightly, avoiding language that sounds critical. Even with an accurate assessment, it won't be well received unless paired with an attitude of humility and compassion—which my husband demonstrated well.

Scripture highlights the importance of humility in relationships:

- Paul says, "Do nothing out of selfish ambition or vain conceit. Rather, in humility value others above yourselves" (Philippians 2:3).
- Peter says, "Clothe yourselves with humility toward one another, because, 'God opposes the proud but shows favor to the humble'" (1 Peter 5:5).
- James says, "Who is wise and understanding among you? Let them show it by their good life, by deeds done in the humility that comes from wisdom" (James 3:13).

I'm thankful for Randy's humble push toward finding Jamie the help she needed. Diagnosed with an anxiety disorder at the root of Jamie's symptoms, she began counseling. We began our own search for understanding and how we could help.

Two decades later, Jamie is a thriving young adult. She works in full-time ministry, where she disciples other young ladies and works as a mental health coach to those struggling to find their place. Humility paved the way for harmony and healing in our home.

Create a humble heart in me, Lord.
Help me consider others more important than myself.
Give me sensitivity, every day, with my words.

THOUGHT FOR THE DAY

Mature relationships in blended families
require healthy doses of humility.

Loving Your Stepchildren

My command is this: Love each other as I have loved you.

JOHN 15:12

"I love my own children differently than I love my stepchildren; I feel so guilty about it." Sarah agonized over her confusing emotions.

"It's okay," I told her. "Your feelings are normal."

We develop a bond unlike any other when we give birth to our children, nurture them for years, and experience every first with them. It's not unusual to love our stepchildren differently. In fact, in the early years, we might not love—or even like—them some days.

I wanted to offer the same love and grace to my stepchildren that I easily gave my biological children, but it didn't come naturally to me in the beginning. I prayed I would see them through God's eyes, not mine. My heart began to soften as I prayed for my stepchildren by name.

We watch Jesus offer love and grace to others repeatedly in Scripture. In John 8:1–11, we read the story of a woman caught in adultery and brought into the temple courts. The Pharisees and other leaders wanted to have her stoned. But Jesus said to them, "Let any one of you who is without sin be the first to throw a stone at her." Then He turned to the woman and offered His grace without hesitation: "'Neither do I condemn you,' Jesus declared. 'Go now and leave your life of sin.'"

We don't deserve the gift of grace God offers us—nor can we earn it—but He wants us to receive it anyway. Ephesians 2:8–9 says, "For it is by grace you have been saved, through faith—and this is not from yourselves, it is the gift of God—not by works, so that no one can boast."

Some days, we don't want to offer the gifts of love and grace to our stepchildren, do we? Perhaps we feel they don't deserve it. Grace is the key that unlocks tension in stepfamily relationships and allows love to flourish. Prayer gives us the strength and compassion we need to move beyond our selfish nature and offer loving gestures to our stepchildren, even when we don't feel like it.

Prayer changes relationships. Stepfamily relationships may always feel a little different than biological ones, but don't be surprised if you notice a growing love and more natural ability to extend grace toward your stepchildren as you pray for them.

Thank You, Father, for loving me on days I'm not lovable.
Teach me to see my stepchildren as You see them and
love them in the midst of confusing emotions.

THOUGHT FOR THE DAY

Feelings for our stepchildren often change with
time, particularly when we pray for them.

14

The Privilege of a Stepparent

But I know this: I was blind, and now I can see!
JOHN 9:25 NLT

"Please pray for our marriage. I'm afraid my husband is about to walk away." My heart sank as I listened to the voicemail. The woman and her husband had been in our stepfamily class, and I knew their struggles. I hadn't expected her spouse to quit.

The challenges of stepfamily dynamics cripple couples who don't have the tools they need. Yes, it's hard. In fact, it's overwhelming at times. It's not unusual to feel like your stepfamily relationships will never be what you'd hoped. But that isn't reason enough to quit. God walks with us.

I'll never forget when a counselor asked me to consider it a privilege to be a stepmom. Not a right to discipline or an expectation to be loved. A *privilege*. A privilege to impact two children in a way no one else could.

It didn't feel like a privilege. It felt confusing and chaotic. It was harder than I'd ever anticipated. And the rewards, at that point, were sparse. I sensed God wanted me to see that I'd been given the privilege to influence my stepchildren differently from anyone else. Did my stepchildren need me in their lives? No. They had a mom and a dad who loved them dearly. But my extra love, my guidance, my encouragement, my extra nudging them toward Christ—that could make a difference.

We get it wrong when we seek to influence our stepchildren as if we were their biological parents. When we ignore the hurt and loss they've experienced and ask them to love us because we've joined their family. When we expect them to respond to our rules and discipline, although we haven't earned that role.

Do you want to make a difference in a child's life? Do you want to impact the next generation for Christ? You can! In a unique way—God's way. Perhaps from a perspective different than you'd expected, but one just as important.

Changing my heart about my role made it easier. I wasn't responsible for their behavior, so I could lower my expectations. Because the relationships didn't need to look a certain way, I could step back and enjoy them. And, with my new perspective, I could stop taking everything personally, because it wasn't all about me.

Have I done it perfectly? No. But my adult stepchildren love me despite my shortcomings. Am I thankful for the privilege I've been given? Yes!

Give me patience and understanding, Lord, in my role as a stepparent. Show me how to love as You love. Help me recognize the privilege I've been given to influence my stepchildren in a unique way.

THOUGHT FOR THE DAY

A new perspective brings freedom
and joy to stepparenting.

15

Taming the Jealousy Monster

With your help I can advance against a troop;
with my God I can scale a wall.

PSALM 18:29

"I don't know why I feel so much jealousy toward my stepdaughter," said Amanda. "I can't seem to get over it. I know it's affecting my relationship with Danny, but I don't know what to do." Tears spilled down her cheeks as she covered her face.

I reached across the table and took her hand. "The feelings are uncomfortable," I said. "But it's actually normal as you figure out your stepmom role. It's probably linked to fear. Are you willing to talk through it?"

For the next hour, I helped Amanda process her emotions by asking questions—a good exercise to use anytime jealousy shows up. Start with questions like: "Is fear or anger driving my feelings? What am I afraid of losing? What do I feel threatened by? What specific behavior is making me feel jealous?"

When we face the feeling head-on—instead of denying or avoiding it—we can take constructive steps to deal with it. Amanda admitted to feeling jealous when his daughter stayed at their house because of the amount of time Danny spent with her. She felt that relationship took precedence over hers, but she had never expressed her feelings to her husband. An honest conversation (with "I" statements not "you" statements) helped Danny understand how Amanda felt. She asked for a simple gesture of love, like a spontaneous hug or a wink across the room, to help relieve her insecurity on the nights his daughter was there. Danny was happy to accommodate.

As Christians, shame often shows up when we admit to feeling jealous. *If I were more holy, I wouldn't struggle with that feeling,* we think. *If God ruled in my heart, jealousy wouldn't emerge.* The truth is, stepfamily relationships create an environment easily conducive to jealousy. Instead of berating ourselves for a feeling that's normal, let's uncover where it's coming from and ask God to help us move past it.

When we meditate on scripture that reminds us of God's everlasting love, we more easily conquer our feelings of jealousy. "And I pray that you, being rooted and established in love, may have power ... to grasp how wide and long and high and deep is the love of Christ, and to know this love that surpasses knowledge—that you may be filled to the measure of all the fullness of God" (Ephesians 3:17–19).

Heavenly Father, I struggle with jealousy at times.
Give me the courage to face my feelings and understand how
to move past them. Remind me of Your love on hard days.

THOUGHT FOR THE DAY

We can tame the jealousy monster as we work through our feelings and focus on God's unending love for us.

16

Differences Are Allowed

There are different kinds of gifts, but the same Spirit distributes them. There are different kinds of service, but the same Lord. There are different kinds of working, but in all of them and in everyone it is the same God at work.

1 CORINTHIANS 12:4–6

"I got a call from the school again today," said Michelle as we sat down for lunch. "My stepdaughter was the class leader in a silly stunt against her history teacher. Alyssa's always in trouble. I just can't handle it!"

I sat quietly before I replied, "I know. You can't handle it because you would have never done that in school. You were the quiet, compliant teenager. But Alyssa isn't. You're going to have to accept that." Tears pooled in her eyes. I continued, "But also understand that behind her troubling behavior lies a leader. Someone who easily influences others. If channeled in the right direction, God can use that confidence and bold personality in amazing ways."

It's not unusual to have a stepchild whose personality traits differ significantly from our own. It happens with biological children also. We struggle to understand them. We don't recognize their natural strengths because they're not the same as ours. But differences keep life interesting.

In Scripture, God models a love for *all* people, even those who go against His instruction and create their own paths. We see a clear example in Jonah 1. God gives Jonah an assignment: "Go to the great city of Nineveh and preach against it, because its wickedness has come up before me" (Jonah 1:2). But Jonah is afraid. He runs away from God and boards a ship to Tarshish instead.

During a violent storm, Jonah is thrown overboard and ends up in the belly of a fish for three days. Despite his sin, God rescues him. He doesn't turn His back when Jonah makes choices He doesn't like.

We need God's help to love and accept differences with our stepchildren, especially when they go down roads we wouldn't choose. Different personalities create desires unlike ours. We can't dictate the beat our stepchildren march to; they need our encouragement to follow the music they hear.

Our stepchildren need to be understood, not criticized; accepted, and not ostracized. We can encourage them to grow into the persons God created them to be, even when that looks vastly different from who we are.

Thank You, Lord, that not everyone is like me!
But that creates problems sometimes. Give me patience
and understanding to accept others' differentness.

THOUGHT FOR THE DAY

Our stepchildren deserve the freedom to be different.

17

Facing Your Insecurities

Do not conform to the pattern of this world
but be transformed by the renewing of your mind.
Then you will be able to test and approve what
God's will is—his good, pleasing and perfect will.

ROMANS 12:2

I chuckled at her words: "Being a stepmom feels like you're on a seesaw—you're confident one moment, then deflated the next. It brings out insecurities I never knew I had."

If you've been a stepparent for any length of time, you understand her sentiment. Insecurity will reign if you allow it to; it will place itself front and center—especially when you compare yourself to someone else. Perhaps it's your partner's ex, another stepmom who seems to have it all together, or even a friend you envy.

When we compare the brokenness we feel on the inside to the picture-perfect image we see on someone else's outside, it's dangerous. It's not an accurate comparison and results in insecurity.

We overcome insecurity by controlling our thoughts. Paul says: "We demolish arguments and every pretension that sets itself up against the knowledge of God, and we take captive every thought to make it obedient to Christ" (2 Corinthians 10:5). Positive affirmations can replace negative comparisons.

Here are a few positive affirmations that have helped me. Choose the ones you like or create new ones. Say them out loud or to yourself every day.

- I'm fearfully and wonderfully made (Psalm 139:14).
- I am not alone; God loves me (Deuteronomy 31:6).
- I'm strong and resilient; I can rise above (Philippians 4:13).

- I will manage my expectations, so that my expectations don't manage me (Philippians 4:6–7).
- The Lord walks with me and hears me when I speak (Matthew 7:7).
- I'm exactly where I'm supposed to be (1 Thessalonians 5:16–19).
- I will dwell only on positive thoughts (Hebrews 13:6).

We're called to focus our minds on what is right, what is lovely, what is admirable, whatever is excellent or praiseworthy (Philippians 4:8). When I'm struggling with negative thoughts, I turn to the book of Psalms and start with the number that matches the current calendar day. For instance, on March 10, I read Psalm 10 to start and proceed as far as I need. It doesn't take long to find encouraging words and affirming passages to reorient my thinking and renew my mind.

Our thoughts are powerful! Positive words combat insecurity. Let God's love and grace wash over you as you practice encouraging affirmations.

Heavenly Father, I often feel insecure in my new family.
Transform my mind to overcome negative thoughts.

THOUGHT FOR THE DAY

Comparing ourselves to others brings insecurity;
affirming our worth brings confidence.

Pursue Love

*Love never gives up, never loses faith, is always hopeful,
and endures through every circumstance.*

CORINTHIANS 13:7 NLT

"My adult stepdaughter shows no interest in a relationship," Brianna said with a defeated look. "I need help to disengage."

I locked eyes with my friend. "I'm sorry," I said. "Your stepdaughter may not show an interest right now, but that could change in time. I'm not a fan of disengaging."

I hear stepparents throw around the concept of disengaging as if it's okay to quit trying in a relationship. If God has placed you in a stepparent role, you're in a valuable position of influence and support. It will look different in every family—and some stepparents play a more active role than others—but when we seek to disengage, we're usually giving up.

A few years ago, I watched my friend Pamela walk away from her faith for a season. She had been deeply hurt by a relationship that ended, although she had prayed for reconciliation for a long time. She blamed God and began to question His love for her. As a result, she stopped attending church and separated herself from her Christian friends.

Pamela sank into a depression that strangled her happy spirit. I prayed for her and talked to her about the love and grace God offers. He doesn't disengage, even when we reject Him. He gives us free will to make our own decisions about the relationship we want to have with Him. And when we're ready, He opens His arms to us.

We honor the calling God has given us when we follow the same pattern in our home. We engage with love and continue to pursue a relationship in subtle ways. Maybe it's a simple text to check on our stepchild or a comment on a social media post to let them know we care. We don't force ourselves into a relationship when we're being pushed aside, especially with adult stepchildren, but we let them take the lead. And we don't quit trying during seasons when the relationship looks different than we want.

Eventually, Pamela returned to the Lord. When she was ready, she accepted His love and trusted His heart. God didn't hesitate to show His grace.

With God's help, we can do the same with our stepchildren. Give them time. Pray for their heart. And continue to pursue a relationship.

Brianna and her stepdaughter eventually became friends, but it took many years. Brianna's gentle nudges and nonthreatening messages moved them toward a loving relationship.

I want to quit trying, Lord, when I feel rejected.
Give me hope and courage to engage with
love, even when I don't feel like it.

THOUGHT FOR THE DAY

God continues to offer love and grace,
even when we reject Him.

It's a Package Deal

"You of little faith," he said,
"why did you doubt?"

MATTHEW 14:31

"I don't really want a relationship with my stepkids," said Misty, my new client. "I retreat to my room when they're at our house and let my husband deal with them."

I took a deep breath, unsure what to say to the stepmom of two adolescent girls. I knew I needed to tread lightly so as not to offend her. "I understand the stepmom role can be hard and frustrating at times," I said. "But I believe God places us in our stepchildren's lives to provide love, nurture, and a godly influence. Would you be willing to consider another perspective?"

There was silence on the other end of the phone. Then Misty started again. I could hear fear in her reply: "But they don't want a relationship with me either. Why should I pour myself into a relationship with no guarantee of a good ending?"

I asked her, "Have you considered that your hesitancy to form a relationship with your stepchildren will affect your relationship with your husband? He loves his girls. He wants the best for them, and that includes a wife willing to push past her fear of rejection and invest in them."

When we marry someone with children, it's a package. In that package, there's risk. There are stepchildren we might not understand or even like at first. But we can't choose only one part of the deal. It's okay to accept our stepchildren tentatively at first, but we must open our hearts to them.

I'm reminded of the story of Peter, trying to walk on water. He doesn't get it right. He takes his eyes off Jesus and sees the storm. Fear takes over, but as he begins to sink, he yells, "'Lord, save me!' Immediately Jesus reached out His hand and caught him" (Matthew 14:30–31).

There's risk in trying to walk on water. There's risk in investing in stepfamily relationships that might not go the way we want. But what do we gain by choosing to disengage? We'll never find satisfaction in a protected harbor.

The stepparent package includes a spouse and stepchildren. If we choose only the easy part of the package—our reciprocal relationship with our spouse—we'll never experience the satisfaction of a relationship we've fought for.

God will save us when we sink. But we must climb out of the boat and walk onto the water.

Dear Lord, I don't like risk. I want to play it safe in my relationships. But I know that isn't Your will. Give me the courage to move past my fear and reach out to my stepchildren, even if they don't reach back.

THOUGHT FOR THE DAY

Risk is part of the package.

The Stepparent Who Succeeds

"I know the plans I have for you," declares the LORD, *"plans to prosper you and not to harm you, plans to give you hope and a future."*

JEREMIAH 29:11

Early in my writing career, I heard a seasoned writer say, "To take yourself seriously in this profession, you must rise early every morning, get dressed, and move to a writing spot that creates a businesslike atmosphere for yourself." That sounded like good advice. For a long time, I followed those instructions, convinced that doing so would mold me into a good writer.

Perhaps for some, that creates just the right environment. After writing for more than two decades, however, I've discovered that some of my best writing happens while I'm propped up in my bed, wearing unbusinesslike attire. I tuck myself comfortably under a blanket and balance my laptop precariously on my legs, with a cup of coffee at my side. It's not a glamorous sight, but it works well for me.

As stepparents, many of us have read all the books on how to do our role perfectly. We've gone to conferences, listened to others' solutions, and tried to do all the right things. But we still don't seem to measure up. Our efforts aren't producing the results we want, and we've convinced ourselves we're failing.

Success on the stepparenting journey isn't determined by whether we build harmonious, bonded relationships. Success is determined by whether we follow God's plan with a surrendered, devoted heart. In their book *But I'm Not a Wicked Stepmother!* authors Kathi Lipp and Carol Boley write about how we often misjudge our success in a stepparenting role:

Your success does not depend on the outcome of your stepmothering efforts. Your success depends only on those things *you can control*—your attitudes, words, and actions (including the choice to accept God's grace and love). Your success as a stepmother does not—indeed, *cannot*—depend on those things *you can't control*, including the actions of your stepchildren. You can be a successful stepmother regardless of how they think, act, or speak. If stepchildren do turn out well and you have a good relationship with them, you can consider that an added bonus.

Regardless of how our stepchildren behave day-to-day or what decisions they make, we've done our role successfully if we've focused on *our* behavior in treating them fairly, lovingly, and with Christlike attitudes. We succeed when we follow God's guidance with our stepparenting efforts.

Thank You, Lord, for giving me "a hope and a future"
on days when I feel I have failed. Guide my steps
and help me love my stepchildren with Your love.

THOUGHT FOR THE DAY

We succeed as a stepparent when we follow
God's guidance with a surrendered heart.

The Important Role of a Stepparent: Reflect on It

1. Have you accepted the calling God has given you as a stepparent? If not, what steps do you need to take toward that? Will you ask God for a spirit of thanksgiving toward your stepchildren?

2. Do you struggle with jealousy in your stepparent role? Is it linked to fear or anger? Process your feelings with a friend or wise counsel and meditate on Ephesians 3:17–19 to accept God's unconditional love for you.

3. Are your stepchildren different from you? How can you respect their differences and love their uniqueness?

4. Will you accept the risk of loving your stepchildren when you don't know how they'll respond in return? What one step will you take this week to connect with them?

5. What does it mean for you to follow God's plan with a surrendered, devoted heart?

PERSEVERANCE COUNTS

21

Perseverance Wins the Prize

Let us not grow weary in doing good, for at the proper
time we will reap a harvest if we do not give up.

GALATIANS 6:9

In the early years of our marriage, I wondered if we would make it to our next anniversary. Blending four children, grappling with stepparent roles while learning to parent together, finding patience for ex-spouses, and trying to stay afloat with work, church, and community obligations seemed impossible. Now, with almost three decades of marriage behind us, I'm thankful we never quit.

Randy and I often counsel other stepcouples. One day, I asked him why he thinks the divorce rate of blended family couples continues to climb. His answer was simple: they quit too soon. Yes, there are struggles with ex-spouses, complicated schedules, bickering kids, financial concerns, and all kinds of issues. But stepcouples often fail because they don't get through the integration years—they don't work through the kinks of stepfamily life, gain a rhythm in stepparenting, and find unity as a couple. *Perseverance* is a foreign word in too many homes.

Stepparenting is a marathon, not a sprint. If a marathoner begins a race with even a small consideration to quit when it gets hard, he won't finish. When the muscle cramps slow his gait, when the road stretches endlessly, when his breathing labors under the hot sun, and even when others stumble along the way, he has to decide he won't give in to the temptation to stop. The choice is daunting. But pushing through when the road feels never-ending, learning to cope when the cramps set in, and finding a rhythm despite labored circumstances all offer rewards that outweigh the stumbling we endure along the way.

Very few stepfamilies escape what stepfamily authority Ron Deal calls the "wilderness wanderings." Wanderings look and feel different for every stepfamily, but just as the Israelites wandered aimlessly through the wilderness for forty years, you will endure days—and possibly years—of hardship and suffering in your stepfamily. If you don't determine ahead of time that you will persevere when it gets tough, you will be tempted to turn back. You won't find the blessings that accompany your journey in the end. Stepfamily statistics confirm that.

Perseverance requires an intentional choice. And with that choice comes a reward. "You need to persevere so that when you have done the will of God, you will receive what He has promised" (Hebrews 10:36).

If you're trudging through difficult days in your stepfamily, don't give up. Rely on God's strength and power to sustain you—He will see you through to better days.

Dear Lord, I have days when I want to give up, but I'm committed to stay for better or for worse. Give me the inner strength and commitment to persevere through my challenges.

— THOUGHT FOR THE DAY —

Perseverance is an intentional
choice that comes with a reward.

22

Your Marriage Counts!

That is why a man leaves his father and mother
and is united to his wife, and they become one flesh.

GENESIS 2:24

Mom's behavior during her last season with Alzheimer's was erratic and unpredictable. One day, I found an entire batch of muffins stuffed in the blender with the lid on. I located toilet paper in the freezer and car keys tucked away in special places. Most of the time, Dad seemed unruffled by it. He calmly removed the lotion from her toothbrush and applied toothpaste instead. He carried her lipstick in his pocket, so she wouldn't lose it. And he never criticized or corrected her conversation, which made little sense. I watched an unwavering example of love and devotion that lasted sixty-five years, in sickness and in health.

Marriage includes challenges. It requires commitment. And in a blended family marriage, the rewards of your enduring loyalty to your vows often come late in the journey. But you will find blessings along the way when you persevere.

While raising kids in a blended family, you can't afford to put your marriage on autopilot. Hold your partner's hand while you watch your stepson at the soccer field. Smile at your spouse across the room while making dinner. Stop and send a text that says, "I love you," during a busy afternoon at work. Dream about the future while sipping coffee on Saturday morning.

During a rocky season that included months of unending heartache in her blended family, my sister, Jan, said she was especially discouraged one night. Questioning whether they could find solutions to their stepfamily troubles, she asked her husband, Bob, "What do we do now?" Without hesitation, he offered a gentle answer as he stood and walked toward her: "I'm just going to keep on trying."

What a beautiful answer. One day, the kids will be gone. The food fights at the dinner table, the squabbles over who sits in the front seat, the arguments over chores that didn't get done, the lingering smell of dirty laundry that emanates from their bedroom, the late-night car accidents, the curfews that are broken ... those things won't matter anymore. But a marriage that stayed the course will.

"Two are better than one, because they have a good return for their labor: if either of them falls down, one can help the other up. But pity anyone who falls and has no one to help them up" (Ecclesiastes 4:9–10).

Run toward unity. Do the hard work to look at your own issues instead of always assuming it's your spouse who needs to change. Seek professional help if you're stuck in unresolved conflict. But don't quit just because it's hard. Commit to persevere.

Give me the courage, Lord, to work through our blended family challenges and commit to the long haul when I want to quit. Give us wisdom and discernment as we search for answers.

THOUGHT FOR THE DAY

Marriage requires sacrifice and commitment.

23

Victor or Victim?

You, God, are awesome in your sanctuary;
the God of Israel gives power and
strength to his people. Praise be to God!

PSALM 68:35

"It happened again," said Lisa. "She didn't even say hello when I saw her at the game. Why do I try to pursue a relationship with my stepdaughter?"

"How did you respond?" I asked.

"The same way. I didn't acknowledge her."

I paused before responding, choosing my words carefully. I wanted to say, "Who's the adult here? You're playing the victim. You're making it all your stepdaughter's fault."

Instead, I said, "Teenagers have their own issues that influence their behavior. Sometimes, we make it all about us when it has nothing to do with us. We need to make the mature choice—without expectation of a response—even when we don't want to. Try a simple pat on her shoulder with a hello or a smile when you make eye contact. Create small gestures of love that say, 'I want a relationship with you. I care about you.' But don't expect her to respond."

How we react to others determines whether we are a victim or a victor.

A *victim* mentality says *it's not my fault. You make me feel this way. It's so unfair. Nothing I do can change my circumstances or protect myself from mistreatment.*

A *victor* mentality says *I am responsible for my happiness. I will reap what I sow (Galatians 6:7). I'll ask God to help me make mature choices with no expectations in return. I'm not at the mercy of other people's bad behavior; I can set boundaries for myself.*

In John 5:1–9, we find an invalid who had been lying by the pool of Bethesda for thirty-eight years. Instead of finding help to get into the pool, where it's believed an angel stirred the water and provided healing, the lame man blamed others for his position. When Jesus asked him, "Do you want to get well?" we hear the words of a victim.

"'Sir,' the invalid replied, 'I have no one to help me into the pool when the water is stirred. While I am trying to get in, someone else goes down ahead of me.'"

Jesus countered. He said to the man, "Get up! Pick up your mat and walk." In other words, take responsibility for your choices. And verse eight reads, "At once the man was cured."

Like the invalid, when we feel life has been unfair to us and our journey brings challenges, it's easy to fall into the victim trap. But we'll never find joy and contentment there. That only happens when we embrace responsibility for our happiness. We are more than conquerors through Christ (Romans 8:37).

Become a victor!

*Heavenly Father, I don't want to be a victim. Help me
face my challenges and take responsibility for my choices.
I can't do this on my own, though. I need Your help.*

THOUGHT FOR THE DAY

Become a victor! Choose the high road and
take responsibility for your happiness.

24

Faithful Followers
Gain a Positive Return

The fruit of the righteous is a tree of life.

PROVERBS 11:30

Work all day. Fight traffic driving home. Cook dinner. Clean the dishes. Start over the next day. Exercise, grocery shop, attend soccer games, clean house, participate in Bible study—the list goes on. Some days, it feels like it's too much. When do we get a break from the mundane?

Life includes seasons. While raising kids, we're in the season of *lots* of chores and mundane tasks. Can we find gratitude in it? Colossians 3:23–24 says, "Whatever you do, work at it with all your heart, as working for the Lord, not for human masters, since you know that you will receive an inheritance from the Lord as a reward." As a faithful follower, God promises a positive gain in the end. But sometimes, we need encouragement in the middle!

In his book *A Grace Disguised,* Jerry Sittser says, "It is not what happens *to* us that matters so much as what happens *in* us." Sittser experienced great loss on a lonely road one night. A drunk driver, going eighty-five miles per hour, smashed head-on into Sittser's minivan. Without a second's notice, the tragic accident claimed three generations of Sittser's family: his mother, his wife, and his young daughter.

Sittser describes his journey of recovery, which includes the mundane details of raising three young kids, alone. Through his story of grief, however, you won't find a victim looking for pity. You'll find a warrior claiming victory through the grace that can transform us. In one particular scene, he details an arduous bedtime routine with three uncooperative kids. Before the night is over, he says, "Finally I blow up, start to yell, and chase them off to bed. After they are in bed, I regret losing my patience, wish I were a better father, and long for Lynda's presence and help." In his desperation, he explains where he finds hope.

"In coming to the end of ourselves, we can also come to the beginning of a vital relationship with God. Our failures can lead us to grace and to a profound spiritual awakening. Finally, we reach the point where we begin to search for a new life, one that depends less on circumstances and more on the depth of our souls."

When we direct our focus and energy for our choices inwardly—away from our circumstances—a spiritual maturity emerges that finds joy among simple blessings and contentment in the routine details of life.

Direct my energy, Lord, to the simple blessings of life,
even amid the mundane of my circumstances.

THOUGHT FOR THE DAY

Inward focus brings contentment for simple
blessings during mundane seasons.

The Crisis Stage of Marriage

Always be humble and gentle. Be patient with each other, making allowance for each other's faults because of your love. Make every effort to keep yourselves united in the Spirit, binding yourselves together with peace.

EPHESIANS 4:2–3 NLT

"You're not doing anything wrong," I said as my friend commented on the conflict in her home. "You're following the normal progression. You've hit the crisis stage with your new blended family. Hang in there. It'll get better."

Ann thought things should be easier by now. "We just celebrated our two-year anniversary," she said. "I don't understand his kids, and he and I are not on the same page when it comes to parenting, which creates conflict in our marriage. It feels like we're failing."

In the early years as a blended family, you might feel you're failing at times. But when you consider how relationships progress, it's likely you're navigating the crisis stage. Don't give up!

New Faces in the Frame, a workbook created by Dick Dunn to guide remarried couples with children, outlines six stages that stepfamilies often experience. How a family navigates the stages of marriage can determine the success or failure of long-term relationships.

The infatuation stage is first and the easiest to pass through. Many couples at this stage are blind to the difficulties they will encounter as they date and marry. It's not long before things begin to change, however. They move into the questioning phase and wonder, "What have I done?" and "Why did I think this would work?" During the questioning stage of my remarriage, I reflected on how it seemed easier to be a single parent than cope with the daily challenges in our new family. But I had committed to "for better or for worse."

The most critical stage, the crisis stage, comes next. Levels of crisis vary from minor bumps to major explosions, but this stage represents a turning point in which family members seek change. Challenges build until someone reaches for help. It's a productive stage if families confront the problems and find solutions. Though some kinds of crises and pain in a marriage do lead to divorce—especially where abuse or addiction are concerned—most blended family crises can be worked through and will ultimately strengthen the relationships.

A marriage built on faith helps navigate the crisis stage. The couple who prays together, meditates on God's promises, and fellowships with other believers who maintain a healthy marriage focus will find encouragement to keep moving forward. Perseverance is key when crises threaten stepfamily peace. The apostle Paul reminds us, "Don't quit in hard times; pray all the harder" (Romans 12:12 MSG).

Buckle your seatbelt on hard days and look forward to smoother days ahead. With the crisis stage in the rearview mirror, blended family life often gets easier. Until then, have patience and persevere.

Heavenly Father, we're determined to move through the crisis stage successfully. Help us be humble, gentle, and patient with one another, always taking time to nurture our marriage. Thank You for walking with us through every stage.

THOUGHT FOR THE DAY

You may need the seatbelt of perseverance to travel through the crisis stage, but smoother roads are ahead.

Take Care of Yourself

Dear friend, I pray that you may enjoy good health and that all may go well with you, even as your soul is getting along well.

3 JOHN 2

In our first month of marriage, Randy took a ten-day international business trip. We considered asking his ex-wife to help with his kids while he traveled but chose not to. I convinced myself it would be a great time to bond with my stepchildren, even though I was working full-time and managing a household with four children.

I was wrong.

During our intense time together, I quickly became discouraged by uncooperative attitudes. I was often offended by behavior that didn't match my expectations. I didn't think the week would ever end, and when Randy finally returned home, I was emotionally and physically exhausted.

Pride kept me from asking for help before he traveled. I neglected to consider my own needs and took on more than I could manage during a period of significant adjustment. I quickly learned that, without proper self-care, I wouldn't thrive in my blended family.

As Christians, we often value self-sacrifice over self-care. We strive to *do* more (give more, perform more) and *be* more (more faithful, more helpful, more Christlike). But we eventually fail if we only meet others' needs and never our own.

Scripture gives us examples of self-care and rest:

- "The Lord made heaven and earth, but on the seventh day he stopped working and was refreshed" (Exodus 31:17 NLT).
- "Jesus often withdrew ... and prayed" (Luke 5:16).
- "'Martha, Martha,' the Lord answered, 'you are worried and upset about

many things, but few things are needed—or indeed only one. Mary has chosen what is better, and it will not be taken away from her'" (Luke 10:41–42).

The specifics of self-care will look different for each of us. But to build healthy relationships in our blended family and thrive as a parent, stepparent, and spouse, we need to take care of ourselves spiritually, mentally, physically, and emotionally. Prayer and Bible study can redirect our thinking and teach us to rely on One who is wiser than ourselves to meet our needs. Coffee with a friend recharges our spirits after conflict in our home. Physical exercise motivates us to persevere through rough patches. Hobbies help balance negative emotions as we look forward to something we enjoy.

When we choose to slow down in our fast-paced environment, guilt often sets in. We can push past those negative feelings, however, and determine what self-care we need.

Pray about it. Ask for understanding. Be open-minded. Don't let others determine your choices. Today might be the perfect day to sit by the fire with your favorite book and enjoy a cup of java.

Lord Jesus, I'm not good at slowing down. Thank You for Your example. Show me how to take time for rest, prayer, and reflection.

THOUGHT FOR THE DAY

Self-care is not selfish.

Sacrifices Count

Create in me a pure heart, O God,
and renew a steadfast spirit within me.

PSALM 51:10

My chest tightened as I thought about the graduation ceremony taking place. I should have been there. I deserved to walk across that stage with my classmates and accept the diploma for completing my master's degree. But I couldn't make the trip.

Six months earlier, my husband's job had moved us across state lines. I had taken the last two classes needed at a local university. I'd made a trip over to complete my comprehensive exams and had plans to travel back for the ceremony. But then the ice storm came. And I was eight months pregnant with our youngest son. I sent the email to my advisor with a heavy heart: "I won't be there for the graduation ceremony. Please mail my diploma to the address on file."

Sacrifices. *Why did we have to move before I completed my degree? Why did the ice storm happen today? Why? Why? Why?*

The sacrifices we make in our blended families feel unfair, too. *How do I endure the hurt of being excluded from parent-teacher conferences? What do I do about the loneliness I feel in our family? Why do I have to manage the after-school routine?*

I often think about the sacrifices that Mary, the mother of Jesus, made. Her pregnancy with the Holy One began in shame. The controversy that surrounded His ministry must have created conflict for her. And then she watched her son suffer and die on the cross, bearing our sin. How did she endure that?

She knew her sacrifices were required for her calling. Just like ours are. No one else can do the job God has called us to do. As a stepparent. As a spouse in a blended family. As a grandparent to our stepgrandchildren.

Others don't always see the sacrifices we make. But God does. His blessing will come. Paul tells us in Philippians 2:3–4: "In humility value others above yourselves, not looking to your own interests but each of you to the interests of the others." That's sacrifice. We can be assured it pleases God. "And do not forget to do good and to share with others, for with such sacrifices God is pleased" (Hebrews 13:16).

Gracious Lord, my sacrifices are small compared to Yours.
Keep my thoughts and actions in proper perspective.
Help me find joy in the sacrifices of my calling.

THOUGHT FOR THE DAY

God sees our sacrifices, even when others don't.

28

A Grandparent's Love Is Important

Love must be sincere. Hate what is evil; cling to what is good.
Be devoted to one another in love. Honor one another above yourselves.

ROMANS 12:9–10

Step or not, a grandparent's role is special. You get to invest in a child's life and—hopefully—with more wisdom and understanding than your younger self could offer. A stepgrandparent can also help bridge the gap with resistant stepchildren when love for them blooms into something special.

A stepgrandparent's role takes time and energy. It requires a discerning heart. You can't barge into a stepchild's life and automatically assume an active role with their children. You'll need patience and understanding. I was privileged to discuss this aspect of stepparenting with Gil Stuart, stepgrandfather to six and author of *Restored and Remarried*. He says, "Your stepchild is the gatekeeper. Access to your stepgrandchildren keys off the relationship with your stepchild."

Just as you allow the stepchild to set the pace in your stepparenting relationship, you'll need to follow their lead in establishing your grandparenting role with their children as well. Offer love and acceptance. Pray for softened hearts and opportunities for meaningful interactions. And be careful to treat all grandkids the same. "Be sure to love them as your own, not differently than biological grandchildren," Stuart says.

Our perspective often determines our behavior. When we have biological grandchildren in our lives before stepgrandchildren come along, it may be harder to establish fair relationships for everyone. Or if a biological grandparent tries to push us out, we might want to give up the fight. Don't. It's a privilege to love and invest in the lives of stepgrandchildren.

"Love is patient, love is kind. It does not envy, it does not boast, it is not proud.

It does not dishonor others, it is not self-seeking, it is not easily angered, it keeps no record of wrongs. Love does not delight in evil but rejoices with the truth. It always protects, always trusts, always hopes, always perseveres" (1 Corinthians 13:4–7). It's easy to skim over the love chapter or simply apply it to our marriage. But Paul's words give good counsel for stepgrandparents too. Love always hopes. Love always perseveres.

If your stepgrandparent relationships aren't where you'd like, don't give up. Continue to remain hopeful for loving exchange. Persevere through the tension. And ask God to bless your efforts.

Heavenly Father, help me to remain hopeful for loving relationships with my stepgrandchildren. Give me patience and understanding to persevere when the relationships aren't what I desire yet. Soften their hearts to accept me into their lives with open arms.

THOUGHT FOR THE DAY

A loving stepgrandparent helps bridge the gap with a stepchild.

29

Overcoming Loneliness

Two are better than one, because they have a good return for
their labor: If either of them falls down, one can help the other up.
But pity anyone who falls and has no one to help them up.

ECCLESIASTES 4:9–10

A BBC piece shares the story of Florence, a ninety-five-year-old widow in London struggling with loneliness, and Alexandra, a twenty-seven-year-old student looking for affordable housing. They came together as part of a home-share opportunity. The friendship that developed between the two tells a beautiful story about basic human needs.

"I think we all need companionship," said Florence. "It's important to have someone to talk to instead of sitting here looking at four walls and thinking, 'What am I gonna do now?'"

"I have a new friend," said Alexandra, "and somewhere that I can feel safe and not isolated in a really big city." The two ladies, with a sixty-eight-year age gap, make a perfect pair as they help each other deter feelings of loneliness.

Loneliness is a common emotion in blended families. When the marriage relationship suffers as a result of stepfamily adjustments, we feel lonely. When the new people in our home don't invest in everyday communication with us like we want, we feel lonely. Perhaps as Florence did, we need to look for creative solutions.

"Loneliness was the first thing that God's eye named not good," John Milton wrote. God created man after creating all the living creatures. And He recognized something was missing. God said, "It is not good for the man to be alone. I will make a helper suitable for him" (Genesis 2:18).

From the beginning, God created us to be in relationship with one another. We have an innate need to belong and to feel loved by others. In the early years of stepfamily life, when relationship tensions are at their peak, those needs might go unmet within our home.

Church friendships, work associates, prayer partners, Bible study companions, gym buddies, and outside family members can help meet our needs for love and belonging when our tank moves toward empty. In addition, a devoted relationship with the Lord satisfies our deep longing for acceptance as we experience His love and comfort. Paul writes, "I pray that you, being rooted and established in love, may have power, together with all the Lord's holy people, to grasp how wide and long and high and deep is the love of Christ" (Ephesians 3:17–18).

Loneliness subsides and often dissipates as stepfamily relationships integrate. Until that happens, our walk with the Lord and friendships with others outside our stepfamily can help. Experience the beauty of community on lonely days—reach out to others and respond when others reach out to you.

Dear Lord, lead me to healthy friendships. Show me where to find community on lonely days. Fill my tank with Your love every day.

THOUGHT FOR THE DAY

Forming relationships outside our
stepfamily can help combat loneliness.

Push Past Your Limit

With your help I can advance against
a troop; with my God I can scale a wall.

PSALM 18:29

Have you ever reached an exercise threshold where your mind convinced your muscles they were maxed out and couldn't do anymore? The brain plays a deceiving role in convincing our body it's fatigued when, most of the time, we can keep going. Some studies suggest we have as much as 50 percent left in the tank when our brains tell us to stop. With extreme athletes, mental toughness becomes just as important as physical endurance.

I would suggest the same principle applies to relationship building in blended families. We need mental toughness to keep loving and leading faithfully when we want to quit. We can convince our brains to push past the point of exhaustion, even when we think we should stop. Our thoughts are powerful.

Moses relied on the Lord to transform his thinking and push past his limits. God spoke to Moses at the burning bush and chose him to be a savior to His people. Moses took his calling seriously and led the Israelites through the wilderness for forty years. But it wasn't an easy journey.

The Israelites grumbled often. Caught between the advancing Egyptian army and the Red Sea, they cried out in fear to Moses. They said, "Was it because there were no graves in Egypt that you brought us to the desert to die?" (Exodus 14:11). Moses assured them the Lord would deliver them from the Egyptians. Then, the Lord demonstrated His great power with the miraculous parting of the Red Sea. The Israelites crossed over unharmed with a wall of water on each side. Following close behind, the Egyptians drowned when the Lord swept them into the sea.

God's deliverance wasn't enough, however. Not long afterward, the Israelites began to grumble again, convinced they were going to starve to death. Moses' mental toughness showed up. He trusted God, refusing to be persuaded by negativity. He continued to promise that the Lord would provide. And God did.

When grumbles and murmurs in your home threaten your peace, ask God for an extra dose of mental toughness. If you entertain thoughts that the relationships in your stepfamily present too many challenges, you'll likely quit. Your behavior follows what your brain tells it to do. Reprogram your thinking. Allow God to help you push past your limit.

Heavenly Father, I need mental toughness to keep going when I want to quit. Give me an extra measure that enables me to take the high road every time.

THOUGHT FOR THE DAY

We need mental toughness as we build
relationships in blended families.

Don't Quit When Relationships Disappoint You

*Blessed are those who trust in the L*ORD *and have made the
L*ORD *their hope and confidence. They are like trees planted along
a riverbank, with roots that reach deep into the water. Such trees
are not bothered by the heat or worried by long months of drought.
Their leaves stay green, and they never stop producing fruit.*

JEREMIAH 17:7–8 NLT

I'll never forget the incredibly lonely season I endured after we moved to Louisiana. My youngest daughter had just graduated from high school and stayed behind in Arkansas to start college. My oldest daughter and stepson had started college there two years prior. After the move, our youngest became an only child. Our previously active house, full of teenagers and noise, was now silent.

One morning, I drove to a nearby park for a run, hoping it would lift my mood. In my unsettled state, I locked my keys and my phone in the car. I asked to borrow a phone from a stranger on the path and called my husband. "You don't have to come right away," I told him. "I can run a few miles while you finish your meeting."

Three miles turned into four, then five. No Randy. I didn't want to borrow a phone again. I kept running. Finally, after eight miles, I decided Randy had forgotten me. I started the two-mile trek home with tears streaming down my face.

I let myself in through the back door. I then called my husband and got his voice message. Within ten minutes, he arrived at the house with the extra set of car keys. "Gayla, I'm so sorry," he said with tears in his eyes. "I got distracted. Work is really hectic today, but I have no excuse. How can I make this up to you?"

Randy is a great guy. He treats me like a queen. But he'll be the first to tell you he isn't perfect. We laugh about that scene now, but it took me a while to work through my anger.

People will let us down. If we look to our spouse to make us happy, complete us, or fulfill our every need, we'll be disappointed. If we expect our children or stepchildren to behave a certain way, we'll harbor anger or resentment. We live in a fallen world with imperfect people. When others fail us, we're called to forgive and move on.

The Lord Jesus Christ remains faithful. We can trust Him with every circumstance—with every relationship. "Jesus Christ is the same yesterday and today and forever" (Hebrews 13:8).

I've been let down by others, Lord.
Thank You that I can always trust You.
Bring healing and wholeness to my deepest places.

THOUGHT FOR THE DAY

Manage your expectations so they don't manage you.

Perseverance Counts: Reflect on It

1. In what area of your family life do you think the principle of perseverance is most needed? Do you give up easily, or are you willing to push through?

2. Has your family experienced a "wilderness wandering"? How did perseverance show up during that season with you or others in your home?

3. Will you commit to persevere and do your part to connect with a prickly stepchild? What action can you take to help?

4. Read the story of Moses leading the Israelites in crossing the Red Sea in Exodus 14. Consider how Moses showed perseverance with his people and how to apply his example in your own life.

5. How can you use mental toughness to keep going when you want to quit? If you need encouragement, reread "Push Past Your Limit" and ask for God's help.

SEEK WISDOM

Separate Marital and Parenting Issues

Everyone should be quick to listen, slow to speak
and slow to become angry, because human anger
does not produce the righteousness that God desires.

JAMES 1:19–20

"I refuse to get on that bandwagon and stay consumed with his problems," said Jessica. "It's a tough situation, but I don't want it to ruin every aspect of our lives." Wise words spoken by a stepmom coping with the drug abuse of her teenage stepson. The strain of his problems could easily interfere with her marriage to his dad.

"I'm proud to see you separate the difficult parenting issue from your new marriage," I told her. "That's not easy."

In blended families, we often allow hard issues surrounding the kids to bleed over into negative feelings toward our spouse. When I blamed my husband for stressful parenting moments with his children in the early years of our marriage, he said, "I'm your friend in this marriage, not your enemy. We can work this out together. But we have to be on the same side, and I don't sense you're on my team right now."

He was right. I had let kid issues create a strain in our relationship. Although there will naturally be some overlap, we can train ourselves to separate the two if we stay aware of the dynamics. I learned to pray for wisdom as the first step.

Stepchildren carry a lot of power in marriage. When allowed that advantage, they can easily divide a relationship. Frequent dialogue between a couple is imperative to maintaining unity. Sparks might fly at times, but that doesn't indicate failure. Disharmony is normal, particularly during the early years, but we need to attack the problem, not our partner, in the midst of it.

The apostle Paul gives wise advice about our words: "Do not let any unwholesome talk come out of your mouths, but only what is helpful for building others up according to their needs, that it may benefit those who listen" (Ephesians 4:29). My family memorized this verse during our high-conflict years. As we discussed troubled behavior, Randy and I countered our language against thoughts of: "Will my words build up my spouse? How can I say this in a way that will benefit my partner?" When we're careful to avoid offense, we more easily express concerns and move toward resolve without entangling marital and parenting issues.

Dear Lord, I want a thriving marriage, but I need Your help.
Give me wisdom and understanding to say the right thing
in the heat of conflict to build unity with my spouse.

THOUGHT FOR THE DAY

Disharmony is normal; resolve conflict by
attacking the problem, not your partner.

33

Experiences Change Us

Walk with the wise and become wise,
for a companion of fools suffers harm.

PROVERBS 13:20

My heart began to race as Randy reached into the medicine cabinet. He had a pounding headache that he said wouldn't go away. But I couldn't trust that my husband was simply reaching for an over-the-counter medication. Prior experience had left me fearful of medicine—all kinds.

I was raised in a trusting, Christian home. As a young adult, I naturally looked for the best in others. I believed in and trusted friends and coworkers easily. But my first marriage changed me. A manipulative personality taught me I couldn't trust others. Addiction and instability had created fear that was not easily controlled.

I didn't suspect my first-marriage issues would show up in my second marriage. But I hadn't resolved my problem of distrust from previous experiences. I needed help to work through the lingering aftermath of what I'd been through.

I'm a huge advocate of taking every problem to God. I believe strongly in the power of prayer and asking for His help with our struggles. But sometimes, we need a person with skin on. Someone who can help us process our challenges, find solutions, and perhaps offer a hug on a hard day.

It's not unusual to walk into remarriage with what counselors describe as "ghosts of marriage past." Perhaps you've experienced abuse, adultery, infertility, or the devastating loss of a spouse. When we leave our ghosts rattling around in the closet, insecurity follows. We need to identify how the aftermath of past experiences still affects us.

I attended Al-Anon (support for families of addiction) before my first marriage ended to cope with the destruction of his addiction. In my new marriage, I needed help with the smoldering ashes of distrust. Randy and I began counseling early to cope with our ghosts and other stepfamily adjustments.

King Solomon—said to be the wisest man who ever lived—talks a lot about the value of wise counsel in the book of Proverbs.

- "Refuse good advice and watch your plans fail; take good counsel and watch them succeed" (Proverbs 15:22 MSG).
- "Without good direction, people lose their way; the more wise counsel you follow, the better your chances" (Proverbs 11:14 MSG).

Wise counsel comes from many sources, including counselors, but also pastors, advisers, and friends who can offer godly advice. Isolation during times of trouble leads to discouragement. Wise counsel leads to hope for better days ahead.

Dear Lord, I don't like to share my problems with others.
But I need help. Guide me to the right advisers and give me
the courage to be vulnerable as I heal from past wounds.

THOUGHT FOR THE DAY

Seek wise counsel in times of trouble.

34

The Danger of Regret

Therefore, there is now no condemnation
for those who are in Christ Jesus.

ROMANS 8:1

"I wish I could go back and parent differently," Kerry said with a distant stare. "I'd work harder to parent without yelling. I'd offer a softer tone. I'd be less critical of my boys' mistakes."

"I know," I said. "I have regrets, too, especially about my early years as a mom and stepmom to our kids. I didn't offer grace enough. I should have been quicker to compliment and slower to criticize. I wish I'd laughed more and demanded less."

We all carry regrets about our past—even the mistakes of yesterday. But when we heap "should haves" on ourselves, we create shame. We walk in defeat. And Satan wins.

We find success by moving forward. The apostle Paul says, "But one thing I do: Forgetting what is behind and straining toward what is ahead, I press on toward the goal to win the prize for which God has called me heavenward in Christ Jesus" (Philippians 3:13–14).

We can't parent well in our blended family if we continue to berate ourselves for how we should have done things. Just like in our cars—we have a large windshield for what's ahead and a small rearview mirror for what's behind.

Can you imagine Peter's regret after he denied Jesus three times? First, we find Peter saying, "Lord, I am ready to go with you to prison and to death" (Luke 22:33). He seems sincere. He has good intentions. But later in that same chapter, he denies Jesus. "Woman, I don't know Him" (22:57). "Man, I am not [one of Jesus' disciples]!" (22:58). And finally, "Man, I don't know what you're talking about!" (22:60).

Regret follows immediately. "The Lord turned and looked straight at Peter. Then Peter remembered the word the Lord had spoken to him: 'Before the rooster crows today, you will disown me three times.' And he went outside and wept bitterly" (22:61–62).

Here's the important part. After the rooster crowed, "The Lord turned and looked straight at Peter" (22:61). The look. Have you considered what was behind the Lord's eyes? Anger? Compassion? Sadness?

We each answer that question differently. Our core understanding of the Lord's love reaches back to prior experiences, perhaps our own parents' love or judgment, that have shaped our view. For some, the look may be condemning. For others, it may be angry or disappointed. Still others see themselves against a measuring stick that reveals they can never measure up.

I believe Jesus offered Peter a redemptive look. One of sadness yet filled with compassion. One that said, "I love you, despite your sin." A look of mercy.

It's the same look and love Jesus offers us, even in the midst of our regret.

I need Your redemptive love today, Lord.
I often feel regret for my mistakes. Help me
begin again, without condemnation, when I fail.

THOUGHT FOR THE DAY

Mistakes are part of the journey;
forgive yourself and start again.

35

Watch Your Self-Talk

Whatever is true, whatever is noble, whatever is right, whatever
is pure, whatever is lovely, whatever is admirable—if anything
is excellent or praiseworthy—think about such things.

PHILIPPIANS 4:8

What thoughts circle in your head? Have you used encouraging self-talk today, like, *You can do this! Don't get discouraged by his attitude?* Or are you more likely to say things to yourself like, *I'm such a failure. It's no wonder this relationship is a mess?*

We talk to ourselves all day long. Too often, we neglect to consider how the words we say, flippantly and without much consideration, influence our feelings and our behavior. If our stepdaughter lashes out at us, we take her words personally: *Why do I even keep trying in this relationship? I can't do anything right in her eyes.* Stop! We can change our self-talk. Commit to challenge the negative words that float around in your head. Refocus your response: *My stepdaughter doesn't understand me. Her words don't reflect who I am.*

We more easily fall prey to negative and anxiety-based self-talk if we were raised in a critical or negative home. I've said things to myself that I would never say to a friend—or even to an enemy! I have to stop and ask for God's help to "take captive every thought to make it obedient to Christ" (2 Corinthians 10:5).

Jesus said the two most important commandments are "Love the Lord your God with all your heart" and "Love your neighbor as yourself" (Mark 12:30–31). These commandments were "inscribed by the finger of God" (Exodus 31:18).

God instructs us to love ourselves. If we want to follow His commands, we will stop using negative and abusive language in our internal dialogue. Loving self-talk includes, *I'm a child of the King. My identity is not determined by whether my step-child loves me or not. I can respond in kindness, regardless of how another treats me. I won't give my former spouse power over my emotions. I'm important in God's kingdom.*

Paul says, "When I was a child, I talked like a child, I thought like a child, I reasoned like a child. When I became a man, I put the ways of childhood behind me" (1 Corinthians 13:11). Let's put childish ways to rest. Let's talk to ourselves in ways that honor and glorify God—and ourselves!

Dear one, God loves you deeply. When you fully grasp His love for you, your self-talk will change to reflect your true image. "But God demonstrates His own love for us in this: While we were still sinners, Christ died for us" (Romans 5:8).

Heavenly Father, I'm thankful for Your love. Help me put aside my childish talk and accept who I am in You.

THOUGHT FOR THE DAY

Positive self-talk honors our true image in Christ and fosters healthy relationship-building in our home.

36

How to Respond to Failure

Whoever conceals their sins does not prosper, but the
one who confesses and renounces them finds mercy.

I have a friend who has lost more than two hundred pounds. I asked her how she stayed motivated for such an impressive feat. Her answers resonated with me, not only for weight loss but for our stepfamily road as well. Here are a few we can apply:

- Dig deep and make a choice from the start to stay committed.
- Lose the victim mentality—it leads to defeat.
- Push through the terror of failing.
- Don't allow "I quit" in your vocabulary.
- When you fail, give yourself grace, shake it off, and start again.

I especially like her last point, but I would add: when you fail, *repent*. We're going to mess up as we build relationships in our blended family. More important than our failure, however, is how we respond afterward. Repentance is an admission of our sin and a desire to turn from it.

Repentance might include an apology to our spouse or a humble admission of error to our stepchild. Repentance offers a fresh start to relationships.

Throughout the Bible, we find examples of people who failed miserably, yet God used them in incredible ways. King David was one. Described as a man after God's own heart (1 Samuel 13:14), David knew repentance had to follow his failure.

God anointed David king of Israel while he was just a boy. Others imagined God would anoint a different man, one who was stronger. But God said of that man, "Do not consider his appearance or his height. ... The LORD does not look at the things people look at. People look at the outward appearance, but the LORD looks at the heart" (1 Samuel 16:7).

Through Scripture, we watch David make mistake after mistake. He commits adultery with Bathsheba, tries to hide her pregnancy, fails, then arranges her husband's death and marries her himself. Surely he knows the depth of his wrongdoing. However, he continues until he's rebuked. David's response when the prophet Nathan confronts him with the consequences of his sin in 2 Samuel 12:13 demonstrates a godly heart. David simply says, "I have sinned against the LORD." No excuses. No justifications. No wallowing. Just repentance.

Can we do the same? What is our first response when we snap at our stepchild? When we act out of selfish instincts instead of godly character? When we overstep our authority?

The likely response is to justify our behavior or perhaps blame someone else. But God looks at the heart, and He asks for repentance. Straight repentance. Every time.

Dear Lord, I often wallow in self-pity instead of repenting for my sins. I want to be someone modeled after Your heart. Help me be quick to repent and slow to make excuses.

THOUGHT FOR THE DAY

Repentance offers a fresh start in relationships.

37

Should We Have a Mutual Child?

If any of you lacks wisdom, you should ask God, who gives
generously to all without finding fault, and it will be given to you.

JAMES 1:5

"I'm thankful for a beautiful relationship with my stepdaughter," said Noelle. "My husband and I have decided not to have a mutual child. Sometimes my friends try to persuade me differently."

"You don't have to justify your decision to others," I said. "It's a personal choice with unique circumstances for every couple."

Choosing to have a mutual child (often called an "ours baby") is a delicate decision. It's not the right decision for everyone. But for our family, having a mutual child—Nathan—has provided complete joy and fulfillment. Nathan unites our children by providing a blood relationship they wouldn't have otherwise. He is our common thread.

Randy and I were careful not to have another child too soon, however. Stepfamily adjustments consumed our time and emotions with the four children we had already. We didn't consider adding another one to the mix for five years. Then, after much prayer, it felt right for us.

Blended family dynamics are different in every home. At one end of the spectrum is a family that deals with ongoing jealousy and resentment among children and stepchildren—emotions that throw up red flags when considering a mutual child. A divided home can quickly become more divided when kids feel they compete for attention.

The other end of the spectrum includes a family that feels united most days. When children and stepchildren have accepted the relationships within the home and stepfamily adjustments simmer most days instead of boil, a mutual child is more likely to be accepted with minimal conflict. Don't wait for the "perfect season," however; it's unlikely the stars will ever be in complete alignment.

Psalm 127:3 says: "Children are a heritage from the LORD, offspring a reward from Him." God gives us children when the circumstances are right. But sometimes He denies our request. His ways are higher than our ways (Isaiah 55:9). Can we trust Him with the *ifs* and *whens*?

During times of indecision, the most important factor is what's right for *your* family. Are you and your spouse in agreement on the decision? Have you educated yourself on it? Are you comfortable with the impact a mutual child will have on the family? Have you prayed earnestly about this important decision? God gives wisdom and discernment for important decisions when we ask.

Heavenly Father, thank You for Your promise
to provide wisdom for important decisions.
I trust You and Your sovereign guidance.

THOUGHT FOR THE DAY

God gives wisdom and discernment for
life decisions; we only need to ask.

38

Let God Heal Your Hurt

I pray that you, being rooted and established in love,
may have power ... to grasp how wide and long
and high and deep is the love of Christ.

EPHESIANS 3:17–18

"I can't shake this feeling of 'I'm not good enough' that emerged after my divorce," Amy explained. "The cloud of failure hovers over me everywhere I go. I just can't get past it."

I remember that feeling. It's been more than thirty years since my divorce, but a failed relationship lingers far past its ending. No one walks to the altar with the intention to divorce. When it does happen, we feel shame. And judgment. Our self-image plummets.

We begin to recover when we accept God's unconditional love and acceptance, regardless of our past. Divorce or rejection doesn't have to haunt us, creating feelings of inadequacy that never go away. That happens when we choose to let self-pity run the show, when we let ourselves become victims of others' choices.

Don't live in your past. Use it as a story of how you came to be who you are, but don't stay there. We serve a God who offers second chances and who redeems brokenness. A God who loves the underdog.

During my early years as a stepmom, I struggled under the sting of rejection. I wanted instant love from my stepchildren. I let myself believe I would never measure up to their mom. Instead of getting credit for the meals I cooked, the laundry I washed, and the endless carpool trips I made for them, I imagined my stepchildren focused on the times I lost my temper. I imagined they thought I inconvenienced them by bringing my own kids into my marriage with their dad.

Outsider syndrome—I experienced it often. It was as if I appeared in our family photo with a blur across my face—some days, it felt like I'd been cut out altogether. I couldn't force my stepchildren to allow me into their inner circle, but I could commit to taking care of myself anyway.

Date nights with my husband, coffee with a work associate, and gym nights with friends helped me feel accepted. On hard days, I invited God's presence into my loneliness. I found the courage to move through rejection by reminding myself that God loved me unconditionally, regardless of whether or not my stepchildren would ever choose to do so.

Divorce, rejection from our stepchildren, and other heartaches can create the illusion that we're damaged goods. Thankfully, a negative self-image can be repaired. It starts with accepting God's unconditional love. Allow His presence to heal your hurt. And remind yourself of the magnitude of His love every day.

Thank You, Father, that You want to redeem my brokenness.
Help me move past my failure and accept Your unconditional love.

THOUGHT FOR THE DAY

Accept God's unconditional
love and move past your failure.

39

The Value and Vice of Social Media

Blessed are those who find wisdom,
those who gain understanding.

PROVERBS 3:13

I learned of a woman recently whose marriage is in trouble. She's desperate for direction, but instead of arranging a private conversation with a counselor, a pastor, or a wise friend, she turns to a much more familiar venue: social media. She posts to Facebook about her dilemma, revealing personal details and laying out her anguish over whether or not she should stay in her marriage. Not a great way to determine how to move forward, right?

When we use social media to replace face-to-face conversations, we miss out on the value of personal relationship. Facial expression, tone of voice, and other nuances communicate our needs and create bonds with others in a way that doesn't happen when we stay hidden behind a computer screen. CNN published a study in 2017 linking frequent use of social media to perceived isolation in young adults.

Social media isn't all bad. We can Snapchat with our children for casual conversation or comment on their Instagram pictures to show we care about their fun with their friends. But we need a healthy balance.

The apostle Paul offers wise words to help us weigh our choices. "'I have the right to do anything,' you say—but not everything is beneficial. 'I have the right to do anything'—but not everything is constructive" (1 Corinthians 10:23).

How do we determine how much social media is beneficial? Our circumstances help dictate that. An infrequent visitation schedule might warrant more social media contact with our children out of necessity. Relationship building looks different in every home, but face-to-face communication offers more meaningful interaction when possible.

What we model with our own standards sends a message to those around us. If we can't close our Facebook app during dinner, our children learn those "friends" take precedence. If we stare at our phone instead of our spouse, we communicate a priority. Our family needs to experience undivided loyalty to *them*, not the latest conversation on social media.

Remember that saying from years ago: "What Would Jesus Do?" I wonder how Jesus would manage social media. Would He engage with His disciples through Snapchat? Or perhaps would He unwind by scrolling through His X feed after a day of miracles?

We don't have a biblical model for social media. But we have the Holy Spirit to guide us. John 14:26 says, "But the Advocate, the Holy Spirit, whom the Father will send in my name, will teach you all things and will remind you of everything I have said to you."

Help me make wise choices with my use of technology, Lord,
and keep my priorities in the right place. Be my helper.

THOUGHT FOR THE DAY

Face-to-face time offers value in relationships.

40

Stepfamily Dynamics—True or False?

Those who trust their own insight are foolish,
but anyone who walks in wisdom is safe.
PROVERBS 28:26 NLT

"I forget that you guys are a blended family. When I'm around your kids, I never get a sense of "step" in your relationships. You're no different than we are."

My friend's comment surprised me. I had confided in her about a challenge with one of our adult kids and referenced our blended family dynamic. She quickly reminded me that what I described was true for *every* family, not just blended families.

It's easy to blame every parenting challenge on our blended family differences. That leads to feelings of helplessness and discouragement, even though the issue may have nothing to do with that.

My mind flashed back to the years Randy and I spent at home with just our son Nathan. Nathan is an "ours" child. There was an eight-year gap between him and the rest of our kids, which meant we had many years with him as an only child. Our home had a different rhythm during those years; we felt more like a traditional family.

Was everything perfect during those years? No! Nathan was a teenager. Need I say more? Family life is messy—in stepfamily homes and traditional homes. Blended family dynamics are not always the root cause of tension or disconnected relationships. Maybe it's just our sinful nature that follows us around.

What challenges are you facing? Are you quick to think:

This would be easier if I weren't her stepmom.
That relationship will always carry tension because we're a stepfamily.
Our stepsiblings are too different. They'll never get along.
Should we just quit trying and consider divorce?

Confusing emotions are part of stepfamily life, but sometimes, our thinking is off. We need to ask God for wisdom and discernment.

In John 7:24, Jesus says, "Stop judging by mere appearances, but instead judge correctly." Jesus is admonishing the Jews for their harsh judgment of His righteous works of healing on the Sabbath. They were only considering an outward appearance instead of an inward need.

In blended families, we often do the same. We judge according to outward appearances only. If our stepdaughter scowls at us, we take it personally instead of considering she might just be having a bad day. When relationships are tense, we jump to negative conclusions instead of accounting that God's redeeming power can help.

It's easy to make wrong judgments about stepfamily life. But God will give us a discerning heart if we ask.

Heavenly Father, I want to believe the best in others.
Redirect my thinking when it's wrong and guide my steps.

THOUGHT FOR THE DAY

When family life is messy, ask God for a discerning heart.

Seek Wisdom: Reflect on It

1. Is your self-talk positive? Write five affirmations that reflect your true image in Christ and change your internal dialogue on negative days.

2. What regrets do you have because of less-than-perfect behavior in your blended family? Meditate on Philippians 3:13–14 and ask God to help you "forget what is behind and strain toward what is ahead."

3. Do you attribute every challenge in your home to blended family dynamics? Discuss it with your spouse and consider what issues are common to *every* family.

4. Do you carry brokenness from past experiences? Meditate on Ephesians 3:17–18 and look up other passages to reflect on God's unconditional love. Allow Him to heal your hurt.

5. Do you have "ghosts of marriage past" that rattle around in your closet? Consider what they are and where to find wise counsel to help.

BLENDED FAMILY
BLESSINGS

Your Efforts Matter!

You are the God who performs miracles;
you display your power among the peoples.

PSALM 77:14

The handwritten letter that fell out of the envelope, along with a gift, surprised me. My stepson, Payton, hadn't sent a Mother's Day gift in years. I certainly didn't expect the words of affirmation that accompanied it. Payton had never called me Mom, yet the letter began:

MOM!! Happy Mother's Day!!

I wanted to take time and express my appreciation to you as my mother!! You have been there through everything. My first love, my first heartbreak, high school, and college. You've literally been there for it all. Thank you for giving me advice and good examples over the years. Even though I know I pushed back for many years, I now realize I had a great MOM all along. Thank you for always being there for me. Love you, Gayla. Your son.

Tears rolled down my cheeks. Payton is now an adult, and I'd often wondered if my tireless efforts as his stepmom even mattered. The letter I received that Mother's Day told me they had.

I reflected on what an imperfect stepmom I am. I could spend days relaying countless ways I've messed up with my children. I didn't know how to raise a son, and I didn't "study" Payton enough so I could parent him better. But God used my imperfect efforts, and He continues to redeem a less-than-perfect relationship.

If you're struggling in a stepchild relationship that's on a downward spiral, don't give up. God redeems relationships every day. When you're discouraged, pray for guidance, make an effort to foster a healthy relationship, apologize when you're wrong, and keep moving forward amid the obstacles.

"Perfection is not the goal on earth. ... Your life is a progressive journey," writes Dr. Saundra Dalton-Smith in *Set Free to Live Free: Breaking through the 7 Lies Women Tell Themselves*. "There will be times of success and times of failure. There will be times of faith and times of doubt. There will be moments of joy and moments of fear. You cannot maneuver this obstacle course we call life and expect to finish the race perfectly."

Don't underestimate your value with your stepchildren. The stepparenting journey often includes a stride forward followed by a setback, particularly in the early years. But stepparents who choose to stay the course, through the good times and the bad, will make a difference in the lives of their stepchildren and discover rewards along the way.

Heavenly Father, I ask for Your help in my stepfamily relationships. Heal our troubled relationships and show me how to be the stepparent You've called me to be.

THOUGHT FOR THE DAY

God uses imperfect stepparents in miraculous ways.

Thankfulness Is a Perspective

Rejoice always, pray continually, give thanks
in all circumstances; for this is God's
will for you in Christ Jesus.

1 THESSALONIANS 5:16–18

My daughter Jamie spent eight months on a missionary assignment in Mozambique, Africa, after she graduated from college. As I listened to her describe the challenges of those who "live in the bush," I realized how often we take everyday privileges for granted. I'm thankful for hot showers every morning. I'm thankful I can do my laundry in a washing machine instead of a bucket. And I'm especially thankful for a warm house on cold days.

As I reflected on my blessings, I also thought about my thanksgiving for the hard lessons I'd learned through tough stepfamily seasons. After almost three decades of stepfamily life, I recognize how much I have to be thankful for.

- I'm thankful for the choice of loving children I didn't birth and knowing I've positively influenced them.
- I'm thankful for learning the value of perseverance.
- I'm thankful for the beauty of forgiveness and how it changes relationships.
- I'm thankful for the chance to learn what patience looks like in everyday life.
- I'm thankful for second chances, for relationship do-overs.
- I'm thankful for ex-spouses and learning through broken relationships.
- I'm thankful for a husband who didn't give up when I made poor choices.
- I'm thankful for my stepchildren and what they've taught me.
- I'm thankful for the Lord Jesus, who has walked with me every step of my stepparenting journey.

How about you? What blessings have you received as a result of your stepfamily journey? The apostle Paul says, "Devote yourselves to prayer, being watchful and thankful" (Colossians 4:2). Prayer must come first. Then thanksgiving can follow. He says it again in 1 Thessalonians 5:17–18, "Pray continually; give thanks in all circumstances."

Only when we commit our minds and hearts to prayer can we maintain an attitude of thanksgiving in all things.

Heavenly Father, I don't always feel thankful for the tension in our home and our complicated stepfamily dynamics. Give me a fresh perspective for today. Help me find the blessings amid the struggles.

THOUGHT FOR THE DAY

A thankful heart breeds contentment.

43

Co-Parenting Success

*If it is possible, as far as it depends
on you, live at peace with everyone.*

ROMANS 12:18

I watched my son's friend negotiate an upcoming visitation schedule with his dad. I could sense the stress the teen felt as he was caught in the middle between his parents. I wanted to step in and tell the dad, "Call your ex-wife and work this out. It isn't your son's responsibility."

Trying to be amicable with someone you couldn't stay married to doesn't happen naturally. It's easier to ask our kids to handle the communication than deal with our ex-spouse. But it's our responsibility, not our children's, to negotiate the details. Your former spouse might have been a lousy marital partner, but that doesn't automatically make them a lousy parent.

It's important for the emotional well-being of our children that we work through our differences and find common ground in co-parenting. We manage only one side of the equation, but our efforts will influence others. When we place the focus on the kids and follow the Golden Rule to treat others as we want to be treated (see Matthew 7:12), we encourage co-parenting success.

Co-parenting happens more easily when we refuse to keep score, choosing to let go of our pride. Bitterness creeps in if we track every misdeed of our ex or count the unending sacrifices we make that don't match up. We avoid looking at our own faults when we dwell on another's.

Scripture warns of the dangers of pride. "Where there is strife, there is pride, but wisdom is found in those who take advice" (Proverbs 13:10). "The LORD detests all the proud of heart. Be sure of this: They will not go unpunished" (Proverbs 16:5).

We must also let go of the happenings in the other home. Fear naturally shows up when we release control, but we can be assured that God wants what's best for our children. Praying for our kids brings peace.

God provides "fear not" verses from Genesis to Revelation to counter the stronghold of fear. Memorize them for hard days. Meditate on them when you're struggling. Isaiah 41:10 is one of my favorites: "Do not fear, for I am with you; do not be dismayed, for I am your God. I will strengthen you and help you; I will uphold you with my righteous right hand."

Our kids deserve cooperative co-parenting between their parents. The benefits of secure, contented kids are worth the effort.

Heavenly Father, I need Your supernatural help to offer a kind and gentle spirit to my former spouse. I want to do what's best for my kids. Help me to put my pride away and treat my ex in the same way I want to be treated.

THOUGHT FOR THE DAY

We encourage co-parenting success when we focus on the kids' needs and not our own.

44

Celebrate the Blessings

Devote yourselves to prayer, being watchful and thankful.

COLOSSIANS 4:2

Too often, we focus on stepparenting challenges. We get out of bed grumpy, expecting that our stepchildren will misbehave before our day even begins. We spout angry words when a snarly look comes our way without taking a pause to reflect.

Why not assume the best in those around us? Instead of looking for misbehavior, expect to have loving conversations with your stepchildren. Refuse to engage if that doesn't happen. Look for opportunities to praise cooperative attitudes. With God's help, strive to smile more and laugh easily.

Blessings surround us. Sometimes, they're disguised, invisible unless we're intentionally looking for them. Prayer helps us identify the good in our lives and not focus on the less-than-good.

I live in the Deep South, where summers are long and winters are mild. Snow rarely shows up, and no one knows how to drive in the white stuff when it does. School lets out with a prediction of flurries.

My stepson recently moved to Colorado and has been anticipating his first winter there. In October, he sent a picture of a foot of snowfall, marking the beginning of winter in a radically different climate. I could hear his excitement as he described the beauty of the powdery snow, quite different from the sleet and ice normally experienced with a winter storm in the South. I rejoiced with him in my reply, anxious to hear more about his plans to romp around outside.

As I related the conversation to my husband that evening, I celebrated the ease of exchanging drama-free words with Payton. For many years, that wasn't the case. Tension surrounded our relationship. Thankfully, with God's help, we've walked out of that season. I now count our thriving relationship a blessing.

The apostle Paul tells us contentment is not found in the situations of life but rather in our attitude about them. Writing from prison, Paul says, "I have learned to be content whatever the circumstances" (Philippians 4:11). We choose every day to either grumble about our challenges or look for blessings to celebrate.

The stepparent's road has bumps, curves, and potholes. Some seasons stretch out endlessly with dark clouds and rainy days. Rather than asking God to fix our problems, however, let's ask Him to fix our perspective so we can find blessings in each day and a rainbow behind every cloud.

Heavenly Father, thank You for walking beside me day after day. I need Your help to find the blessings that surround me and to carry an attitude of thankfulness despite my circumstances.

—————— THOUGHT FOR THE DAY ——————

Gratitude for our blessings brings joy.

45

We Serve a God of Order

God is not a God of disorder but of peace.

1 CORINTHIANS 14:33

My friend's frazzled look gave away her troubled heart. Words tumbled out when we crossed paths at the grocery store. "I had no idea what I was getting into with my blended family," she said. "It just feels so chaotic at our house. A schedule I can't keep up with, expectations I can't control, and too many kids making demands I can't fulfill. Please tell me this gets easier!"

I gave her a hug and offered some reassuring words. I remember the angst I felt when my family with two kids mushroomed overnight into a family of four. I didn't know how to be a stepmom or wife in my new marriage. The demands on my energy and emotions overwhelmed me. I craved order in our home, but I couldn't stop the merry-go-round of craziness.

With multiple children and not-easy-to-manage routines that include kids traveling back and forth between homes—sometimes multiple homes—we can't control the chaos. But we can control how we react to it. Chaos doesn't have to reign in our hearts, even if it sometimes rules in our homes.

Psalm 119:37 says, "Turn my eyes away from worthless things; preserve my life according to your word." The writer, David, asks God to help him live according to His ways. He wants to ignore worthless distractions that surround him and bask in God's magnificence—the higher calling of God's ways. We can do the same. We can turn our eyes from the worthless distraction of chaos and preserve our life by focusing on His ways—His promises, His power, His peace.

Writer Rita Schiano says, "Talking about our problems is our greatest addiction. Break the habit. Talk about our joys." Perhaps in stepfamily life, talking about the chaos is our greatest addiction. We ruminate over the out-of-control schedule, the ex-spouse's unpredictable temperament, or the moodiness of our stepchild that contributes to the chaos. Can we break the habit? Can we talk about our joys?

Yes, we can! We can ask God to turn our eyes away from worthless things and focus on His magnificent ways. We can talk about our blessings. We can bask in God's presence, no matter what we face. We will then have peace in our heart, even when there's chaos in our home.

I need Your help, Father, to turn my eyes away from the chaos in my home and focus on the peace and joy I find in You. Show me how to create order in our home and find contentment on days when I feel out of sorts.

THOUGHT FOR THE DAY

Chaos doesn't have to reign in our heart,
even if it rules in our home.

46

Blessings Abound

Let perseverance finish its work so that you may be
mature and complete, not lacking anything.

JAMES 1:4

"Who will walk the girls down the aisle when they marry?" my ex-husband asked.
I cringed. I knew he was concerned about the relationship that had developed between our two daughters and their stepdad, Randy.

"We will do what the girls want to do," Randy replied. *A brilliant response,* I
thought. Fast forward ten years. My youngest daughter, Jodi, was the first to marry
of our five kids. A few months before the wedding, she broached the subject with
Randy. "Dad, I'd like you to walk me down the aisle. You're the one who's been there
for me."

Always my steady-Eddie, Randy has walked through both the good and the bad
with my two girls. Beauty pageants, band concerts, cheerleading events, maturing
attitudes—but also temper tantrums, adolescent meltdowns, parking lot fender-
benders, late-night phone calls, teenage drama, failing grades, and so much more.
Thankfully, Randy never walked away.

After twenty years of stepparenting, Randy experienced an unexpected blessing—well-deserved by a man who's given unselfishly to his stepdaughters. Not perfectly, though. Randy will be the first to tell you he's done a lot of things wrong as a
stepdad. But the girls know his heart. As young adults, they see his good intentions.

I know it doesn't always happen that way. Stepfamily weddings can be awkward
and less than joyous. If you've experienced that with your stepchildren, I'm sorry.
There will be other blessings among the challenges on your journey. Simple things.
A smile from across the room. A request for your opinion on a sensitive issue. A
light-hearted evening that includes laughter and hugs with your stepchild.

Hebrews 12:1–2 says, "Let us run with perseverance the race marked out for us, fixing our eyes on Jesus, the pioneer and perfecter of faith." The race you're running is different than mine. The blessings you experience will be different than my husband's. But if your eyes are on Jesus, you'll find them. Expect them. Look for them. Experience the joy of today, not the regret of yesterday or the fear of tomorrow.

Above all, let grace and mercy prevail in your home. And then bask in your own unexpected blessings of stepparenting.

Heavenly Father, I want to discover the unexpected blessings of my stepparenting role. Open my eyes today so I can see what I'm missing.

THOUGHT FOR THE DAY

When you persevere in your stepparenting role, you will discover unexpected blessings.

47

We Find Freedom in Boundaries

Show me your ways, Lord, teach me your paths.
Guide me in your truth and teach me, for you are
God my Savior, and my hope is in you all day long.

PSALM 25:4–5

I didn't grasp the power of boundaries until well into my adulthood. I rarely considered my own needs because I was too busy looking out for the interests of others. Smothered in an alcoholic marriage for eleven years, however, I finally learned how to set boundaries, to protect myself and free myself from the control of another.

Without boundaries, we're enslaved to one another, victims of our circumstances. That's not God's way. God offers freedom in our relationships. The apostle Paul gives instructions on the value of boundaries to free us from control: "It is for freedom that Christ has set us free. Stand firm, then, and do not let yourselves be burdened again by a yoke of slavery" (Galatians 5:1). Relationships rooted in freedom allow love to thrive.

In a stepparent role, we often chase after a love relationship with our stepchild. We become entangled with their behavior, making endless sacrifices that allow loose boundaries and keep us enslaved. We fail to recognize the freedom we have to make choices that limit the way someone else's behavior affects us.

My stepmom friend Denise resents the endless demands of running carpool for her stepson to basketball practice, after-school tutoring, and church youth group. "I'm crabby every afternoon and snappy with my stepson when I have to spend another day in the car," she told me. "I have a flexible work schedule, and my husband expects me to carry the load."

Enslaved to the demands of others, Denise will eventually resent her stepson and her husband unless something changes. It's her responsibility to express her needs. A conversation with her husband could go something like this: "Honey, I want to help with Joshua's after-school activities, but it's wearing me out. I need your help to find other carpool options for one or two days to give me a break. If that's not possible, we need to make changes to Joshua's schedule."

God designed us to live in freedom. Boundaries help define what that freedom looks like. If we give up too much of ourselves to meet others' needs, a victim mentality with frustration and resentment sets in.

Setting boundaries doesn't mean we become selfish and concerned only with ourselves; it simply means we find a healthy balance with boundaries that fit.

Dear Lord, I want to experience freedom in my relationships. Please help me determine how to make choices that please You and fit my circumstances.

THOUGHT FOR THE DAY

Boundaries offer freedom to
make choices that fit our needs.

48

Celebrating Love

Let love and faithfulness never leave you;
bind them around your neck, write them on the
tablet of your heart. Then you will win favor
and a good name in the sight of God and man.

PROVERBS 3:3–4

I couldn't help but laugh as I read the description of our family, written by our mutual child, Nathan. I'd come upon his elementary schoolwork while cleaning out his closet, and the paper titled "My Family" caught my attention. He wrote:

> We are a family of seven. I have no full-blood brothers or sisters. I have a brother named Payton and three sisters named Jamie, Jodi, and Adrianne. Jamie and Jodi have the same mom as me but a different dad. Payton and Adrianne have the same dad as me but a different mom. Jamie and Jodi are stepsisters to Payton and Adrianne. My family is complicated, and few people understand us, but it's my family.

Nathan is now twenty-three, and he's about to get married. He no longer considers our family complicated—he's accepted the differentness of his sibling relationships. Over time, love among the stepsiblings, half-siblings, stepparents, and stepchildren has grown to feel very similar to what traditional families experience. We will always be a blended family, but we no longer carry the shame of brokenness.

Our relationships aren't perfect. I've written about pride, selfishness, resentment, anger, and other sin-filled behaviors that have crept into our home at times and created havoc and dissension. But we continue to chase after progress, not perfection. We know with God's help, lasting love can be attained; we'll never stop pursuing it.

God's love can transform relationships. It's perfect, all-encompassing, faithful, enduring, redeeming, sacrificial, grace-filled, unconventional, and so much more. It offers mercy when we fail, it gives us hope to keep going, and it moves relationships toward progress.

What does progress in a relationship look like? An act of kindness, a joke at the dinner table, an offer to help, a smile across the room, an apology, or an unexpected phone call.

During a relationship-building season with my adolescent stepson, Payton called me one morning from school. "Did you know our county is under a tornado warning, Gayla?" he said. "You might want to take cover."

I never expected Payton to think of me during that precarious event. His act of kindness didn't go unnoticed. I thanked Payton for his thoughtful gesture, and I praised God for the progress in our relationship.

Chase after progress, not perfection, as you pursue loving stepfamily relationships. Thank God as you watch your relationships grow and mature.

Guide my steps, Lord, toward acts of love
and kindness to others in my family.

THOUGHT FOR THE DAY

Chase after progress, not perfection, in your relationships.

Unexpected Blessings

All hard work brings a profit, but mere talk leads only to poverty.
PROVERBS 14:23

"It's easy to look back now and realize the blessings of blended family life," Sydney said. "Ten years ago, I doubted whether we would make it to another anniversary. But today, our big, blended family enjoys time together as often as we can. My advice to others on this journey is that you can expect to walk through challenges in the beginning. But time and effort will pay off. Learn all you can about stepfamily life, invest in your relationships every day, stay positive when you're discouraged, pray for God to soften hearts toward one another, keep your marriage a priority, and get counseling if you get stuck, but never consider divorce. If our family has made it this far, others can make it too."

Good advice from Sydney. As I reflected on her words, I thought about blessings from my own life—what God has taught me and how He has grown me up in ways I'm forever thankful for and continue to carry with me. Here are a few:

An Ability to Persevere:
Newt Gingrich says it perfectly, "Perseverance is the hard work you do after you get tired of doing the hard work you already did." Different than in a first family, stepfamily relationships require more effort than you want to give at times. Even then, they might not be the relationships you envision, but if you keep moving in a forward direction, you will bask in the satisfaction that you persevered when it would have been easier to quit.

The Skills to Fight Fair:
Disharmony shows up in relationship building. Unfortunately, I didn't know how

to manage conflict and fight fair. Counseling helped Randy and me learn better communication skills and how to resolve issues by attacking the problem, not the person. I also better understand my own needs and when I need to step away, spend time with God and His Word, and reflect on how to respond to disagreements.

How to Savor Joy in the Moment:
I no longer consider whether I've had a good day or bad; instead, I reflect on where I found joy in my day. Interactions with others in our family can go from hot to cold in a matter of seconds. Maybe your stepdaughter loves your idea of how to celebrate her birthday, but moments later—after a phone call with her mom—ridicules the suggestion. We can choose to take it personally and get mad or move on to another idea. Joy is found in the moment when we recognize loyalty toward a biological parent and move past it without hurt feelings. Unpredictable situations have taught me to embrace moments of love and laughter when they happen and stay flexible with whatever shows up.

A Trust in the Lord That Never Wavers:
Stormy days are part of the blended family road. But God walks with us. Our faith deepens as we seek Him and trust Him to light our path and guide each of our steps. Consider your perspective. Look for the rainbows in the clouds and the blessings in the trials.

Precious Lord, help me to find the rainbows in the clouds.
Thank You for lighting my path and guiding my steps.

THOUGHT FOR THE DAY

God uses our blended families to grow us.

Rewards Will Come

Walk in obedience to all that the LORD your God has commanded you, so that you may live and prosper and prolong your days in the land that you will possess.

DEUTERONOMY 5:33

I smiled as I gazed at the family photo from my daughter's wedding. Our five kids had arranged themselves randomly for the picture. My stepson and daughter stood next to my husband. My youngest daughter and stepdaughter stood on each side of me with our youngest son on the end. The picture reflected a beautiful blending of relationships after more than twenty years as a stepfamily.

Family pictures looked different in our early years. My two girls always stood next to me, and my husband's son and daughter stood next to him. Mingling of his kids and mine didn't happen in those photos. Although our two families were joined through marriage, the lack of relational bonding showed up in how our children placed themselves.

I'm thankful for the growth and maturing of our kids' relationships. Introductions of each other no longer include stepsister, stepbrother, or half-brother—only sister or brother. With the passing of time and experiences together, our family has developed loving, lasting bonds as strong as any traditional family—it's a blessing my husband and I cherish.

Rewards in blended families come in all shapes and sizes. We often need to carry a discerning heart to recognize them: laughter around the dinner table, an observation of a wise choice that results from your guidance, a hug in a public setting or an unexpected gift from your stepchild, more harmony in your marriage, an apology for misbehavior, or a family photo that tells a new story.

In the early years, rewards might not come as soon or as often as we'd like. We're doing our part in relationship building to extend love and acceptance, but we're not receiving the same gestures in return. Regardless of the response of others, we can be assured our heavenly Father sees our behavior and will offer a blessing for our efforts. Proverbs 3:3–4 says, "Let love and faithfulness never leave you; bind them around your neck, write them on the tablet of your heart. Then you will win favor and a good name in the sight of God and man."

Blessings follow a faithful and obedient heart. We gain the best reward for our efforts when we hear, "Well done, good and faithful servant!" (Matthew 25:21).

Heavenly Father, help me stay obedient to the calling
You've given me in my blended family. Give me eyes
to see the blessings I overlook or take for granted.

THOUGHT FOR THE DAY

Your efforts will bring a reward.

Blended Family Blessings: Reflect on It

1. What rewards have you experienced in your blended family?

2. Do you consider even the small rewards? Hugs, laughter, random texts from a stepchild, and late-night conversations are all blessings.

3. Have you discovered the power of gratitude in uncovering the blessings of your family? Take a moment to reflect and name three things you're grateful for in your relationships.

4. How do you need to change your behavior to chase after progress, not perfection, in your relationships?

5. Reflect on the blessings of how God has used your blended family journey to grow you.

THE BEAUTY OF GRACE

51

Your Spouse Needs Grace, Too

Out of his fullness we have all received
grace in place of grace already given.

JOHN 1:16

Money was tight for our family of seven for many years. We could always count on more bills than money at the end of the month. But Randy never questioned my desire to stay home, work flexible jobs (that made little money), and pour into our quiver of kids the best I could. His grace overshadowed our deficiencies.

Marriage creates complex dynamics in a blended family. As a stepparent and a biological parent, I understand both roles. Your spouse faces an uncomfortable struggle when torn between you—the stepparent—and his or her child. If a decision has to be made without time to consult you first, or a prickly ex-spouse changes the visitation schedule with little notice, it's easy to feel irritated or angry toward your spouse. Or perhaps you feel your spouse supports your stepchildren over you and looks out only for their best interests. Jealousy easily creeps in.

Your spouse isn't always going to say or do things the way you want. Feelings get hurt. Unkind words are said. I encourage you to take the high road when it happens. Offer grace and mercy—even if you feel your partner doesn't deserve it. None of us deserve the grace God offers. But He gives it to us anyway.

We enjoy being recipients of God's love and grace, but treating others the same way doesn't happen easily. We're quick to point out our spouse's faults but slow to offer grace. We nitpick behavior that we don't like but fail to consider our own shortcomings.

Second Peter 3:18 tells us to "grow in the grace and knowledge of our Lord and Savior Jesus Christ." Growing in grace means to mature in our Christian walk, becoming more and more like Christ Jesus. It means we work harder to please and obey God. We move away from our sinful ways and closer to righteousness. Growing in grace paves the way for a healthy, thriving marriage.

After an extended trip out of state recently, I discovered a traffic violation while fumbling through the mail on my return. I fumed as I saw the license plate of my husband's car attached to the fine for running a red light. *Another ticket,* I thought. *Always running by the seat of his pants. Geeeez!*

I quickly snapped a picture and sent an indignant text to my husband. "Really? Again?" Within minutes, I received a reply. "Did you notice where that happened? It's out of state. You took my car, remember?"

I felt my face flush. He was right. How did that happen? I must have neglected to see the camera on the light that captured my driving error. Before my fingers could start an apology, I received another text from my husband. An emoji with a smiley face. Then, a heart.

No words—just a beautiful expression of grace from a man who looked past my errant ways.

Thank You for the love and grace You show me, Lord.
Help me offer grace and mercy to my spouse, freely and often.

THOUGHT FOR THE DAY

Grace is the light that adds sparkle to a marriage.

52

In Their Shoes

Don't look out only for your own interests,
but take an interest in others, too.

PHILIPPIANS 2:4 NLT

One of my biggest downfalls in the early years of our blended family was my inability to consider the roads others in my family were walking. My own road felt so complicated as a mom and stepmom to four kids navigating my new marriage as a part of a stepcouple, working full-time, and managing a back-and-forth household with two former spouses. My main objective focused on how to get to the next day with stable emotions and a peaceful heart. And many days, I didn't do that well.

Over time, I began to recognize that our kids—all four of them—had their own hard journeys. I became more compassionate to my stepchildren who navigated a schedule that included living in two homes. Emotions were unsettled at times as they missed their mom when they were with us and missed their dad when they were with her. And all the kids in our home had to adjust to a new stepparent and two new stepsiblings, some of whom shared a bedroom together.

There was a birth order change for my girls. My oldest daughter, Jamie, was a big sister to her younger sibling, Jodi. But my stepdaughter, Adrianne, became Jamie's big sister, and Jamie lost her birth order. For a strong-willed, independent child, that was a big deal to Jamie. Sparks between Jamie and Adrianne ignited often.

While I adjusted to my new role as a stepmom, our kids adjusted to their new role as stepchildren. I can now see and understand the feelings my stepchildren must have experienced. They loved their mom dearly, which naturally created conflicting emotions toward a stepmom. Author Lauren Reitsema has said it best in her book, *In Their Shoes: Helping Parents Better Understand and Connect with Children of Divorce:* "My stepmom's character was acceptable to me; however, the role she now played was not. My stepmom is, and always has been, kind, gracious, generous, and supportive, yet for many years, my responses to her rarely mirrored these virtues. It was her position that threatened acceptance, not the person she was."

Accepting a new stepparent doesn't feel natural. When I learned to "walk in their shoes," I gained deeper compassion and understanding when uncooperative attitudes showed up. I more easily offered grace for behavior that felt like rejection. And I had a stronger desire to continue striving for loving, trusting relationships with my stepchildren.

It took me too many years to change my mindset—to consider the needs of others in our home with a humble spirit. I pray you don't make the same mistake.

Heavenly Father, I want to change my selfish ways. Help me understand the journey others walk and the burdens they carry. Give me a heart full of love and grace for those in our home.

THOUGHT FOR THE DAY

When we walk in the shoes of those in
our home, we gain deeper compassion
and a heart full of grace for them.

53

One Day at a Time

Do not worry about tomorrow, for tomorrow will worry about itself. Each day has enough trouble of its own.

MATTHEW 6:34

"My anxiety heightens as the holiday season gets closer," said Jessica, a new step-mom. "I don't want to face the inevitable. I have to see my husband's ex-wife at every holiday concert; find time to shop and figure out what gifts to buy my hard-to-please stepchildren; make the schedule work with the extra back-and-forth routine; act like I care about my in-laws when they visit ... it's just too much. I wish we could skip it altogether."

Holidays with stepfamily dynamics create complicated scenes. I've been there—year after year—with five kids and crazy schedules. I can't control much of what happens. But I *can* control how I respond. When I commit to live one day at a time, life becomes more manageable.

God gives grace and provision for today, not tomorrow. When the Israelites wandered in the wilderness for forty years (Exodus 16), God supplied manna each day. A supernatural gift, it appeared on the ground each morning except for the Sabbath. Although freely given by God, the people had to gather it. On the sixth day of the week, they were to gather a double portion since the manna wouldn't be provided on the Sabbath, a day of rest. If they gathered more than a daily portion on any other day, it spoiled.

It's the same with us: God doesn't give us strength or courage to face tomorrow until we get there. He provides what we need today. When tomorrow comes, He'll meet our needs again.

Grace and flexibility become part of unwrapping holiday peace one day at a time. When the agreed-upon schedule must suddenly be changed, flexibility prevents anger. When our stepchild needs a gift for his teacher that the other parent promised to provide or the costume required for the school play doesn't show up with our stepchild's belongings, grace prevents heightened emotions.

Our stepkids need additional grace as they adjust to divorce, remarriage, and strangers in their new family. Routines change during the holidays, creating uncertainty and unsettled emotions. With a one-day-at-a-time attitude, we more easily offer grace. It's the perfect answer when irritability, sadness, or a stubborn demeanor show up.

We create problems for ourselves when we jump out of today and into tomorrow. Leo Buscaglia offers a good reminder: "Worry never robs tomorrow of its sorrow, it only saps today of its joy."

Thank You, Lord, for giving me the strength
and courage I need for whatever I face. Help me
stay focused on today until tomorrow comes.

THOUGHT FOR THE DAY

When we live life one day at a time, we find peace.

54

Don't Sweat the Small Stuff

Hatred stirs up conflict, but love covers over all wrongs.
PROVERBS 10:12

"Please pray for us. My stepdaughter tried to commit suicide. We've just arrived at the psychiatric hospital." I shuddered at the text that appeared on my phone. My friend lived out of state, and the best I could offer was a virtual hug and promises of my thoughts and prayers.

Within a few hours, I received a text from a different friend. "My stepson is driving me crazy. He's the pickiest eater I've ever met. How do you deal with this stuff?"

I closed my eyes and said a quick prayer. I didn't want to send a condescending response. But what I wanted to say was, "Really? You're allowing a picky eater to drive you crazy? Can I tell you about a friend who's struggling with a *real* problem?"

Blended family life includes varied annoyances, like messy rooms and loud-mouthed teenagers. They'll grind on our last nerve if we let them. We often have little tolerance for our children's petty behavior, which escalates for attention when they don't feel loved or accepted by us. Russell Barkley is known for saying, "The kids who need the most love will ask for it in the most unloving ways."

We can look past the small stuff when we keep the ultimate goal in mind—healthy, loving relationship building—while we focus on working for the Lord in all that we do. Paul says it best in Colossians 3:23–24: "Whatever you do, work at it with all your heart, as working for the Lord, not for human masters, since you know that you will receive an inheritance from the Lord as a reward. It is the Lord Christ you are serving."

You've likely heard the expression: "Is this a hill to die on?" In other words, is what you're fighting about really important? I'm not suggesting we never raise a flag about issues that bother us. However, particularly when we parent teenage children in blended families, we should carefully consider whether we want to battle every issue or extend mercy.

When we consider the long view—that we want to raise mature, Christ-minded adults—we are more likely to make the right choice with our kids and stepkids. And when we *do* draw a line in the sand, like insisting our stepchildren attend church when they're in our home, it's best to let the biological parent lovingly enforce the standard.

I need help looking past the small stuff, Lord.
Give me the tolerance and patience I need to develop
loving relationships with those in my home.

THOUGHT FOR THE DAY

When we overlook minor annoyances, we're
more likely to build loving relationships.

55

Your Newfound Normal

Let your conversation be always full of grace, seasoned with
salt, so that you may know how to answer everyone.

COLOSSIANS 4:6

"Her body is starting to shut down. There isn't anything else we can do. I suggest you place her on hospice care." The doctor's words didn't surprise me. Mom had been declining for days. Actually, years. She had courageously battled Alzheimer's for more than a decade. But as she entered the last days of her life, tears often spilled down my cheeks. I wasn't prepared to say goodbye.

Life without Mom has forced my dad, sisters, and I into a newfound normal. Confusion and tension show up as we make decisions about how to distribute her belongings or where to celebrate holidays. Grief hurts. Disharmony compounds it.

On hard days, I make an intentional effort to offer my family grace. I remind myself of the pain each of us carries without Mom in our lives. I don't always get it right, but I make an effort to live at peace with everyone, as far as it depends on me (Romans 12:18).

Blended family life also creates a newfound normal. Some days, that normal includes joy, peace, and contentment. Other days, it includes frustration, sadness, and confusion. How do we respond to those around us as we navigate uncomfortable emotions?

A few years into our marriage, my parents celebrated their fiftieth wedding anniversary. The celebration was a large family gathering, and I wanted my stepchildren to attend. My teenage stepdaughter, who was living with her mom in another town, resisted. When my husband wouldn't insist she be there, I became angry with him. She was the only grandchild not at the celebration, and it took me a long time to understand his reasoning on that issue.

My husband sees the long view better than I do. Insisting his daughter endure an obligatory family celebration wasn't necessary. Maintaining an amicable relationship with her during a tough season was.

Our stepchildren are trying to navigate their own newfound normals. We can encourage peaceful exchange when we extend love and grace to them. Grace softens rough edges. It gives others the courage to love. Even when we feel they don't deserve it, grace is the right answer.

Heavenly Father, I don't always want to extend grace to others. But I'm reminded of Your ultimate sacrifice and grace You extended to me, undeserved. Give me the courage to offer grace to my stepfamily today.

THOUGHT FOR THE DAY

Offering grace during times of
heightened emotions encourages peace.

56

Shame Paralyzes

And the God of all grace ... will himself restore you
and make you strong, firm and steadfast.

1 PETER 5:10

"Are they twins?" The dreaded question came up during church camp signup. "No, they're stepsiblings." I felt my face flush as, once again, I explained how we had two children six weeks apart in age who weren't twins. With divorce as part of my story, the familiar feeling of shame followed.

"What we don't need in the midst of struggle is shame for being human," says research professor Brené Brown. Although I know that in my head, my heart doesn't always get the message. My story can still bring shame, especially when talking to churchy people.

Shame showed up often for me as a stepmom. I couldn't get it right. I blamed myself for tense relationships. If I were a better stepmom, my stepchildren would love me more. If I had more patience, we'd have peace in our home. Shame. It seemed to follow me.

It took a long time for me to accept God's grace and step out from under the mantle of shame. I had to reprogram my thinking. I had to change my self-talk. I had to memorize God's promises and then claim them when shame threatened to take me down.

Here are a few verses that have helped:

- "Let us then approach God's throne of grace with confidence, so that we may receive mercy and find grace to help us in our time of need" (Hebrews 4:16).
- "God, in his grace, freely makes us right in his sight. He did this through Christ Jesus when he freed us from the penalty for our sins" (Romans 3:24 NLT).

- "You created my inmost being; you knit me together in my mother's womb. I praise you because I am fearfully and wonderfully made" (Psalm 139:13–14).

I wish I could say I no longer struggle with shame. I do. But God doesn't call me to be perfect.

Even when I've done something wrong, like yell at my stepchild or try to manipulate my husband, God's mercy covers my behavior. He loves me too much to let me wallow in shame. He even gave me the beautiful last name of Grace when I remarried to remind me of His grace every day. What a gift!

Thank You, Lord, for Your grace and mercy. Help me accept it and plant it in my heart. Remind me that I'm fearfully and wonderfully made on days I don't feel that way.

THOUGHT FOR THE DAY

When we accept God's grace and mercy,
we stop shaming ourselves for our imperfect ways.

57

A Gracious Heart in Co-Parenting

And do not bring sorrow to God's Holy Spirit by the way you live.

EPHESIANS 4:30 NLT

"Seriously?!? You want me to maintain a gracious heart with my ex-husband? That sounds like an oxymoron to put gracious and ex-husband in the same sentence!"

I wasn't surprised by my friend's reaction. Desiree had been feuding with her ex since her divorce proceedings started years prior. Now, she and her former spouse were trying to parent together, and it wasn't going well. She asked for my help.

"I know. I get it," I said. "I also have an ex-husband who I believed, for many years, did not deserve grace. But would you consider doing it for the sake of your kids? They've been through enough: divorce, remarriage, a new stepdad, stepsiblings, a new school, a new house, heartache, uncertainty. I could go on and on. They don't deserve more pain by witnessing a contentious relationship between their biological parents."

Desiree nodded her head with an understanding look. "I guess. You're right. But it sure isn't easy."

She's right. It isn't easy. We need God's help to be gracious toward a former spouse. And if we repeatedly struggle with it, we might also need to check our hearts. Are we carrying resentment from unresolved wounds? Do we keep the pot stirred with a disagreeable attitude, believing nothing will ever change with them and the relationship will always be prickly? Do we harbor resentment?

My former spouse went down the road of addiction during our marriage, and huge consequences followed. I held onto unforgiveness far too long. Until one day, God spoke to me through Scripture. "And do not bring sorrow to God's Holy Spirit by the way you live. ... Get rid of all bitterness, rage, anger, harsh words, and slander, as well as all types of evil behavior. Instead, be kind to each other, tenderhearted, forgiving one another, just as God through Christ has forgiven you" (Ephesians 4:30–32 NLT).

Ouch ... I needed the Holy Spirit's help daily with hard blended family dynamics. And I asked for it. Yet, I was grieving His heart with my behavior. Bitterness was a constant feeling toward my former spouse, as were harsh words and slander. That day, I was convicted of what a sinful, broken person I am and how desperately I needed forgiveness on a regular basis. How could I be prideful enough to neglect offering forgiveness to my former spouse?

If we want to maintain a gracious heart toward our former spouse, we will likely need to wrestle with forgiveness. And for the sake of the kids, it's an important consideration, following the guidance Scripture gives us.

Heavenly Father, I'm undeserving of the grace and forgiveness You show me daily. Thank You for the reminder to offer it to others. Give me the courage and willingness to maintain a gracious heart with my former spouse.

THOUGHT FOR THE DAY

Co-parenting with a gracious heart requires God's help.

58

The Gift of Flexibility

Do nothing out of selfish ambition or vain conceit. Rather,
in humility value others above yourselves, not looking to your
own interests but each of you to the interests of the others.

PHILIPPIANS 2:3–4

"It doesn't seem fair that we always have to change our schedule to accommodate the kids based on her plans," complained Anne. "My husband will rarely challenge his ex. He just gives in and goes with it."

"I'm sorry," I said. "You might not be able to change that, and I know it's frustrating. But remember—when you offer the gift of flexibility, you also offer love and grace to your husband. I'm not saying you guys should always be the ones to bend, but a father who doesn't have custody of his kids may feel threatened by the power the mom holds. Perhaps he's afraid to buck her too often."

When we choose to bend with the changes that naturally accompany the back-and-forth schedule, we prevent breaks in our relationships. Like the trees in our backyard, the ones that bend under windy conditions break less often.

Jesus models flexibility throughout Scripture. He heals the sick and the crippled when the need arises, even on the Sabbath. He follows the direction of the Father, even when it goes against the norm of the culture. When the Pharisees complain about the disciples "working" on the Sabbath by plucking heads of grain and eating them, Jesus disregards their criticism in His reply: "There is far more at stake here than religion. If you had any idea what this Scripture meant—'I prefer a flexible heart to an inflexible ritual'—you wouldn't be nitpicking like this" (Matthew 12:6–7 MSG).

Inflexibility is rooted in pride—we consider our ways more important than another's. Sometimes, we feel entitled to ask others to make provisions for us. Scripture tells us repeatedly that we reap what we sow. Paul offers an explanation in Galatians 6:7–8 (MSG): "The person who plants selfishness, ignoring the needs of others—ignoring God!—harvests a crop of weeds. All he'll have to show for his life is weeds! But the one who plants in response to God, letting God's Spirit do the growth work in him, harvests a crop of real life, eternal life."

Flexibility requires God's Spirit to do "growth work" within us while He builds our character. And blessings will follow, as Paul tells us in the next verse: "Let's not allow ourselves to get fatigued doing good. At the right time we will harvest a good crop if we don't give up or quit" (Galatians 6:9 MSG).

Heavenly Father, I often have an unbending spirit.
Help me look beyond my own needs and wants
and offer flexibility to those around me.

THOUGHT FOR THE DAY

The gift of flexibility shows love and
grace in blended families.

59

Moving Past Defeat

*Therefore, if anyone is in Christ, the new creation
has come: the old has gone, the new is here!*

2 CORINTHIANS 5:17

"At the end of each day, I'm exhausted and still worried I'm not doing it right or even good enough." The mom's words resonated with me. I remember those feelings. It took me years to allow God's grace to overcome my guilt.

Sometimes, we *don't* get it right. We let our sinful nature take over instead of walking with the Spirit (Romans 8). We don't work hard enough to love our stepchildren, or we overlook the annoying tendencies of our biological children. We highlight our children's mistakes instead of praising their successes.

Our kids desperately need to feel that we love them. A wise counselor once told me, "We accept the love we think we deserve." If our children and stepchildren don't feel loved and accepted in our homes, it will be harder for them to embrace love as an adult.

But we don't have to wallow in guilt over mistakes. It's natural that some days we don't feel like loving those in our home. Their habits, their language, their disrespect—it's too much. I know. I understand. But we can't get stuck there. Our kids deserve more than judgment or condemnation. In the midst of our sin, Christ offered us everlasting love.

When Paul talks about us in 2 Corinthians, he describes us as a new creation. We aren't some kind of a side project or a fixer-upper that God tweaks and updates when He feels like it. We are a new creation. Just like God created the world with miraculous power in Genesis, He has done that same type of work in you.

It is so easy to look at our lives, and only see what we have done, entirely missing what God has done. While our sins do need forgiveness, God doesn't stop there.

The new life He has created in us has changed us, giving us the spiritual strength and stamina to grow and to love, even in hard times.

God's physical creation is amazing, and we marvel at star-filled nights or the roar of the vast ocean. But on those days when we feel the weight of shame and despair, we can remember that we are a *new* creation. We are God's *magnum opus*. This truth doesn't erase our mistakes, but it can certainly put them in context!

God wants to do "immeasurably more than all we ask or imagine, according to His power that is at work within us" (Ephesians 3:20). But we have a part to play—allowing His grace to wash over our guilt.

Heavenly Father, the messages in my head don't always line up with the ones in my heart. Help me to accept Your grace and Your mercy to move past my defeating thoughts.

THOUGHT FOR THE DAY

Grace triumphs over guilt.

Grace Bestows Blessings

But to each one of us grace has been given as Christ apportioned it.

EPHESIANS 4:7

We own an obnoxious cat named Trixie. My daughter Jamie brought her home one night and asked if we could keep her temporarily. Her friend had found her behind a garbage dump as a kitten, but she was leaving for college break and needed a temporary place for her to stay. We agreed. Her friend never returned, and Trixie joined our family.

Cats are cantankerous. But this one is like no other! Trixie has a reputation. Even the vet talks about her contrary disposition. She excuses it, however, because Trixie was a stray. "She was never taught social skills by her mom," the vet says. "You have to look past her ill-mannered ways."

Really? We're supposed to excuse her behavior because she was a stray? It makes me think about the difficult situations many of our stepchildren experienced before they entered our lives. Perhaps we should be better at looking past their "ill-mannered ways."

Trixie doesn't know how to play nicely. She bites and hisses and squeals when Randy plays with her. But it doesn't keep him from trying to engage over and over. He chooses not to let her obnoxious ways offend him and doesn't take her behavior personally.

As stepparents, we're often quick to assume our stepchildren's behavior translates to an attack against us. We're certain our stepdaughter is mad at us when she walks in from school and throws an ugly look our way. Perhaps someone was mean to her on the bus ride home. We wonder what we've done wrong when our stepson goes straight to his room after he arrives from the other home. Maybe he's simply sad about leaving his mom for a week.

Here's a motto I've tried to follow with my stepchildren: *Give them the benefit of the doubt until you discover otherwise.* Look past their ill-mannered ways; offer grace and mercy frequently. Don't assume their behavior has anything to do with you. Maybe it does. But more often than not, it doesn't.

First Corinthians 13:7 says: "Love never gives up. ... [It] trusts God always, *always looks for the best*, never looks back, but keeps going to the end" (MSG, emphasis mine). When we "always look for the best," we give another the benefit of the doubt.

God looks past our offensive ways. He doesn't hesitate to offer grace, even when we don't deserve it. He asks His children to do the same.

Heavenly Father, thank You for the grace You offer me every day. Help me to give others the benefit of the doubt more freely and offer grace more readily.

THOUGHT FOR THE DAY

Grace sets the stage for relationships to flourish.

The Beauty of Grace: Reflect on It

1. When was the last time you offered grace to your spouse? Are you more likely to keep track of their offenses, like when they neglected to support your stepparent role, or they catered to their former spouse? Consider your spouse a gift and offer them grace today!

2. Do you struggle with the shame of divorce? Or feeling different from others at church because you're part of a blended family? Accept God's love and grace. Meditate on scripture to help: Hebrews 4:16, 1 Peter 5:10.

3. Extending grace to a former spouse isn't easy. But for the sake of the kids, it's important. Do you need to wrestle with forgiveness first?

4. What blessings have you experienced as a result of grace? Offer your stepchildren the beauty of grace and watch your relationships flourish.

5. As believers, we experience God's grace daily. Who needs an extra dose of grace in your family today?

COPING WITH GRIEF

61

When Grief Strikes

In all these things we are more than conquerors through him who loved us.

ROMANS 8:37

I noticed Amber's melancholy state when I met her for lunch. "I was excited about a new beginning in marriage," she said, "but now I find myself sad more often than happy. I'm not sure why."

As we spoke further, I recognized the problem. Amber's vision for a new beginning included a "white picket fence" that never went up and expectations that never came to pass. She had envisioned peaceful meals around the dinner table and fun times at the ball field as she cheered for her stepchildren. She had neglected to consider the teenager who smacks his food every night and the awkwardness of the ex-spouse who sits a foot away in the bleachers. She had prepared herself for a period of relationship bonding but hadn't accounted for endless months of sassy attitudes, slammed doors, and late-night meltdowns.

Blended families often have expectations that don't take form. Sometimes, we need to step back and reevaluate. Amber needed to grieve the loss of *what she'd hoped for*—her white-picket-fence life that didn't materialize. Her unfulfilled expectations were creating feelings of disappointment and sadness. "Embrace your loss," I told her. "Feel the ache of what might never be. Rely on your faith on sad days."

We don't have to bear our grief alone. We can claim promises from God's Word to help us on troubled days. Here are a few of my favorites:

- "The LORD is close to the brokenhearted and saves those who are crushed in spirit" (Psalm 34:18).
- "Blessed are those who mourn, for they will be comforted" (Matthew 5:4).
- "He heals the brokenhearted and binds up their wounds" (Psalm 147:3).

Jesus wants to comfort us when we're troubled. We watch Him minister to Mary and Martha, sisters of Lazarus, after their brother's death. John 11:33 says Jesus was troubled and deeply moved by Mary's grief. As both God and human, Jesus understands our emotions. We can call out to Him in our distress.

Grief in blended families shows up through loss but also through expectations that never come to pass. When we recognize and name our feelings of sadness and discouragement, we can then turn to God's Word for comfort and counsel. God promises to provide a way in the wilderness and water in the wasteland. In John 16:33, Jesus says, "In this world you will have trouble. But take heart! I have overcome the world."

New beginnings often include loss. But when we move forward through our troubled circumstances, we will find we are indeed more than conquerors through Him who loves us!

Comfort me during times of grief, Lord.
I need Your help to be a conqueror today.

THOUGHT FOR THE DAY

New beginnings often include loss, but God walks with us.

62

When Joy and Sorrow Collide

Weeping may stay for the night,
but rejoicing comes in the morning.

PSALM 30:5

"I wanted to be married again," said Lynn. "When I met Tyler, it had been almost ten years since Bob died, and all I could see were the benefits of having a partner again. I had no idea what challenges lay ahead."

Lynn and Tyler were both widowed when they met at a work social. A friendship quickly developed, and within six months, they were talking about marriage. Lynn had two teenage stepchildren, but Tyler had never had kids.

Lynn and her kids lived in a different town from Tyler, and the kids had little time with him. "Tyler's such a likable guy, I'm not concerned," Lynn said. But, after they married and lived in the same house together, the reality of how her kids felt surfaced quickly. They weren't interested in having a stepdad and didn't care to spend time with him.

Lynn was heartbroken. She just knew that once her kids got to know Tyler, they would love him the same way she did. Grief showed up again. She thought about how easy life had been with the kids before Bob died. Sure, when she and Tyler were alone together, she felt loved and thankful for another chance at marriage. Then, she felt guilty for being happy when her kids were unhappy. How could she balance both emotions?

In Scripture, we find joy and sorrow side by side. In John 16:20 (NLT), Jesus says, "... you will weep and mourn over what is going to happen to me, but the world will rejoice. You will grieve, but your grief will suddenly turn to wonderful joy." Jesus knew there would be terrible sorrow over the events of the cross, but that same event would bring rejoicing for us.

The sorrow and grief that surround blended family challenges are real. But there is also the joy of new beginnings and better days ahead. Don't feel guilty about your good days and the joy that follows. Grieve your losses and celebrate your victories. Allow them to coexist—it's part of the healing process.

Lynn began to accept her children's unhappiness and ask questions about how she could help. They wanted more time with their mom without Bob around all the time. She grieved with them and the changes that had taken place. At the same time, she held onto the joy of her new marriage. She and Bob considered new ways for him to form relationships with her children. The dynamics in her home weren't perfect, but she knew God had orchestrated their steps, and "weeping may stay for the night, but rejoicing comes in the morning."

Lord Jesus, help me accept joy and sorrow as part of my journey right now. Comfort me on sad days and rejoice with me on good ones.

THOUGHT FOR THE DAY

We can experience joy and sorrow together;
allowing both to coexist is part of our healing.

63

Character Building Brings Benefits

We know that suffering produces perseverance;
perseverance, character; and character, hope.
ROMANS 5:3–4

"I would give anything, *anything*, to be in a nuclear family." I could hear the pain behind the stepmom's post on a Facebook page. Several comments agreed with the stepmom's sentiment. A wave of sadness rolled over me.

Really? I thought. *I disagree. I would never trade the experiences I've had with my stepfamily—or the person I am now because of them.*

I began to type my own response to the post. "There are problems in nuclear families, too. I'm thankful for my big, imperfect, blended family. After more than two decades together, we have stories of loss, disharmony, and tears. But we also have stories of love, acceptance, and joy. We have a history together that makes us inseparable. Thankfully, we can now look back on our early years of tension with laughter and understanding."

The trials we've walked through in our stepfamily have kept me on my knees. I've developed an enduring faith because of the magnificent ways I've seen God work. I've learned how to live out the fruit of the Spirit: love, joy, peace, patience, kindness, goodness, faithfulness, gentleness, and self-control (Galatians 5:22–23 NLT). I more easily offer grace and humility to others, recognizing my own imperfect ways. And I've learned to trust God beyond my ability to understand. "For the LORD is good and His love endures forever; His faithfulness continues through all generations" (Psalm 100:5).

The apostle Paul spoke of this same principle. He said, "I was given the gift of a handicap to keep me in constant touch with my limitations. Satan's angel did his best to get me down; what he in fact did was push me to my knees" (2 Corinthians 12:7 MSG).

In the story of Ruth, however, Naomi took a different approach. She blamed God for the loss of her husband and two sons. "'Don't call me Naomi,' she told them. 'Call me Mara [which means bitter], because the Almighty has made my life very bitter'" (Ruth 1:20).

There's only one letter difference between *bitter* and *better*. Bitter contains "I." When we focus on ourselves, our hardship, our unmet desire to live in a nuclear family, bitterness follows. But when we focus on God's provision, God's strength, and the hope found in God's promises, we allow adversity to make us better.

It's our choice.

Heavenly Father, I admit—some days I feel bitter because of my circumstances. But I don't want to stay there. Help me see the blessings of my journey. Remind me of Your goodness and faithfulness.

THOUGHT FOR THE DAY

Our experiences make us better or bitter.

64

Change Requires Adjustment

God is able to bless you abundantly,
so that in all things at all times, having all that
you need, you will abound in every good work.

2 CORINTHIANS 9:8

I clearly remember the first fall season after our family moved from Arkansas to Louisiana. I had struggled with the transition and told my friends I wasn't adjusting well to Lousy-anna. I'd found one saving grace—the beautiful Bradford pear tree in the front yard of the home we'd bought. I had admired the gorgeous display of color from my neighbor's tree in Arkansas and couldn't wait to experience it in my own yard now!

With the first cold snap of the season, I began to watch our tree with great anticipation. One day, I noticed a few leaves at the top of the tree changing color. I knew that someday, very soon, the tree would be enveloped in beautiful red leaves. As if Christmas were approaching, I waited and watched impatiently.

A week later, the tree looked just the same. A week after that, still no change. I began to wonder if our tree was defective; I could count on my fingers the number of red leaves against the backdrop of green.

Disappointment set in. I had convinced myself we would be the envy of our neighbors with the most beautiful tree on the block. It didn't happen. The rest of the leaves never changed color, and within a few short days, the leaves began to drop. I was devastated. My unmet expectation added to my disgruntled attitude with Lousy-anna. Would I ever adjust to this foreign climate?

We lived in Louisiana for more than ten years. Our tree rarely produced red leaves in the warmer climate, but my disappointment faded. I knew what to expect and accepted it. If I wanted to savor fall foliage, my husband and I took a road trip!

We can apply that lesson to stepfamily life. It helps to be mindful of our expectations. If we anticipate that a second chance at marriage will include a white picket fence and everything we missed out on the first time around, we'll be disappointed. If we create images in our heads of a big, happy family that doesn't include adjustments to an unfamiliar climate, we've deceived ourselves.

I'm not suggesting remarriage won't bring joy and contentment. But just like my move to Louisiana, you'll have to give it time. Adjust your expectations. Seek the Lord; find comfort in His Word on hard days. And when you need a drink of refreshment from the mundane, take a trip with your spouse and find some beautiful fall foliage.

Thank You, Lord, for the change of seasons. Help me remember that with change comes adjustment. Help me find contentment, even in the midst of unsettled emotions.

THOUGHT FOR THE DAY

Don't let unmet expectations derail you!

65

Waiting on God

*Take delight in the L*ORD*, and he will give you the desires of your heart.*

PSALM 37:4

I impatiently considered the need for a new phone when mine began to freeze for no apparent reason. My teenage son tried to help, complaining about how long the YouTube video took to load.

We live in a culture unaccustomed to waiting. Deliveries from Amazon Prime in 24 hours or less, microwaveable meals, and TV shows we can DVR to skip commercials all promote instant gratification.

Too often, we expect the same timetable in life circumstances. A coaching client complained recently about how long it was taking to bond with her stepdaughter. "I've worked really hard to form a caring relationship with her, but it's just not happening. I don't know what I'm doing wrong."

"How long have you been married?" I asked.

"Four months," she replied. I looked down at my hands, smothering a smile. I considered how to tell her she could expect it to take at least four years. Some experts say the relationship between a stepmom and her stepdaughter is the hardest because of the dynamics between a daughter and her own mother.

God often requires us to wait on Him for the desires of our heart or answers to life's challenges. Consider the story of Abram and Sarai (later named Abraham and Sarah) that begins in Genesis 12. Twenty-five years pass before God fulfills His promise to Abram that he and his wife will have a child. Sarai gets tired of waiting and takes the matter into her own hands.

Sarai tells her husband, "The LORD has kept me from having children. Go, sleep with my slave; perhaps I can build a family through her" (Genesis 16:2). Surprisingly, Abram obeys. He sleeps with Hagar, and she conceives. That doesn't make Sarai happy, though. She resents her slave and blames Abram for his wrongdoing. "You are responsible for the wrong I am suffering," she says (Genesis 16:5).

What a complicated mess, created by Sarai's impatience. How often do we do the same? Impatient to have a loving, bonded relationship with our stepchildren, we jump into a Super Stepparent role. We buy them gifts, do their laundry, cook their favorite meals, fret over just the right thing to say, help with homework—all in an effort to be accepted into their circle. But it doesn't guarantee we'll clinch the position. Our stepchildren will love and accept us when they're ready. On their terms.

God fulfilled Sarai's longing for a child. He will fulfill the desires of your heart, too. In His time.

You know the desires of my heart, Lord. Give me patience to wait on Your perfect plan in my life and my stepfamily.

THOUGHT FOR THE DAY

God's timing is often different than ours.

66

Moving Past Grief

But if we hope for what we do not yet have, we wait for it patiently.

ROMANS 8:25

"You're not my mom! I don't have to obey you!" Jenny recited a hard scene with her stepdaughter, Brenna. Her brow furrowed as she expressed the hurt and anger that followed.

"I didn't know how to answer her," she said. "I went to my room in tears. A month later, it still hurts to talk about it."

Jenny's stepdaughter, Brenna, had lost her mom suddenly to breast cancer. Jenny had lost her husband to cancer ten years prior. A relationship had developed quickly with Brenna's dad after his wife passed away because Jenny was already friends with the family. Within less than a year, the two were married.

Jenny was excited about love again and a new beginning. She and Brenna got along well prior to the marriage. But when Jenny moved in, everything changed. Brenna wasn't ready for anyone to step into her mom's shoes. When she lashed out at Jenny, she was really saying, "I miss my mom. I don't want anyone trying to take her place."

Blended families come together after loss. Divorce, death, or any relationship breakup leaves holes and hurt. If we plunge forward without resolving the grief left behind, we endure more loss and create unrealistic expectations. We must be aware of our own grief, but also that of our stepchildren. They have their own deep-seated fears and other confusing emotions to work through. Pushing a new stepparent relationship before they're ready adds to unresolved grief.

We find hidden feelings with our stepchildren when we look behind the words we hear and dig into the nonverbal language we see expressed. I'm convinced, as the saying goes, that God gave us two ears and one mouth, so we'll listen more and talk less. James 1:19 reminds us, "Everyone should be quick to listen, slow to speak, and slow to become angry."

In the early stages of relationship building, we can take cues from our stepchildren, just as we do our biological children. If they hug us, we hug back. If they're standoffish, we don't encroach on their space. A gentle attitude with a good dose of patience will encourage our stepchildren to open their hearts when they're ready.

King Solomon offers wise words on the power of patience in Ecclesiastes 3: "There is a time for everything, and a season for every activity under the heavens ... a time to weep and a time to laugh, a time to mourn and a time to dance ... a time to embrace and a time to refrain from embracing ... a time to be silent and a time to speak" (verses 1, 4–5, 7).

Take time to listen; pay attention to the cues your stepchildren send. Then, experience the blessings of your efforts as you watch budding relationships grow and mature.

Heavenly Father, give me large doses of patience and wisdom as our stepfamily relationships develop. Remind me to talk less and listen more.

THOUGHT FOR THE DAY

A good dose of patience allows stepfamily relationships to grow and bond.

67

It's Okay to Be Different

The Spirit of God has made me;
the breath of the Almighty gives me life.

JOB 33:4

Chills ran down my spine when I heard the doctor's words. "You've tested positive for the Alzheimer's gene." *What?* I wasn't even aware he'd ordered that test. *I'm not sure I want to know that*, I thought. My mind quickly went to disturbing images of Mom in her last season with the horrible disease.

As I drove home, I considered what to do with the news. *I'll just keep it to myself*, I thought. *What will others think if they know I'm headed down a road of cognitive decline?* An Alcoholics Anonymous slogan crossed my mind: "We're only as sick as our secrets." I'm all too familiar with the demise of addicts who live in denial of their disease and deceive others to cover it up. Denial leads to darkness. Light exposes our imperfections, forcing us to get help when we need it.

In our new marriage, we didn't always want to admit we're a blended family. It's easier to cover it up than go into the explanation of divorce, stepchildren, loss, and brokenness. When we try to hide our past, however, shame creeps in. Secrets set us up to fail. We want to act like a traditional family, but we're not—we never will be. We can't present that pretense to others.

It's okay—we don't have to hide our differentness. Scripture teaches us that as believers, we're called to be different. We strive to talk and act differently than our nonbeliever friends and coworkers. We seek to live a life that reflects holiness and purity. First Peter 1:15 says, "But just as He who called you is holy, so be holy in all you do."

When we accept that it's okay to be different, we're more likely to walk in holiness and have compassion for others in our stepfamily. We don't have to criticize our stepchildren because they behave differently than we expect. We're less likely to condemn a former spouse who conducts themselves in a way we don't understand. We view others through a lens of understanding, not one of judgment.

I've decided that I don't have to hide the imperfect gene I've inherited. I've accepted the influence it carries, but it doesn't define me. The same applies to our blended family journey. Ours might be different than the road our neighbor walks, but it doesn't define us in a negative light. We're all defined the same as Christians—children of the King who are precious in His sight.

Help me, Lord, to accept my family's differentness on days when I want to hide it. Shine Your love deep into my soul and remind me I'm a child of the King on days when I feel less than others.

THOUGHT FOR THE DAY

God's love defines us, and nothing else does.

68

Where to Find Contentment

Now, Lord, what do I look for? My hope is in you.

PSALM 39:7

Do you create expectations in your mind of how you want your relationships to look? Maybe you're pining for a stronger relationship with your stepchild, or you want your spouse to be more attentive to you.

I've had countless conversations with stepmoms trying to achieve Super Stepmom status, as though there's an end-of-the-year award. They cook their stepchildren's favorite meals, run them around town to every activity, spend hours hunting for the perfect birthday gift, contend with disgruntled attitudes, and neglect their own needs to fulfill their stepchild's every wish.

These stepmoms have an expectation attached to their behavior. They expect their good deeds to win over their stepchild's love. And when it doesn't happen, they're devastated.

Stepchildren develop relationships with their stepparents on their own timetables. Sometimes, our behavior can influence this, but often, it won't. When loyalty conflicts exist (loving a stepparent feels disloyal to their biological parent) or another parent actively seeks to undermine the stepparent's influence, relationships form slowly. Sadly, we can't change that.

It's natural to feel disappointed when your efforts don't produce the results you want. Maybe you've prayed for stronger, more harmonious relationships or a more attentive spouse, and nothing has changed. Expecting something from God that might not happen only results in anger and frustration. We divert our attention away from reality and onto what we expect. Ultimately, we create a god out of our expectations when we dwell only on our desires.

Romans 8:5–6 says, "Those who live according to the flesh have their minds set on what the flesh desires; but those who live in accordance with the Spirit have their minds set on what the Spirit desires. The mind governed by the flesh is death, but the mind governed by the Spirit is life and peace." To live in contentment requires that we allow our minds to be controlled by the Spirit, not our fleshly desires.

Perhaps your expectations as a wife include a husband who regularly dotes on you. Or you thought your stepparent role would include unity and harmony in your relationships. But that isn't happening. Contentment might feel like a far reach.

Contentment isn't based on our situation; it comes through our relationship with the Lord as we experience Christ's sufficiency. There's no need to pine for a spouse who meets our every need or a stepchild who adores us. Sure, that would be nice, but we don't look for contentment there.

We discover contentment when we stop focusing on our expectations, accept our present reality, and trust God to be all we need.

Thank You, Lord, for Your promise of contentment.
Help me take my eyes off my circumstances and put
my trust in You to meet my needs, not someone else.

THOUGHT FOR THE DAY

We live contented lives when we allow our minds to be controlled by the Spirit, not by our human desires.

69

Don't Waste Your Sorrows

Anyone who wants to come to him must believe that God
exists and that he rewards those who sincerely seek him.

HEBREWS 11:6 NLT

"It was to be a Thanksgiving that would change our lives forever."

So begins Carla McClafferty's book *Forgiving God*, in which she unveils the tragedy that left her young son lifeless. On a sunny afternoon in their backyard, fourteen-month-old Corey fell out of a swing and suffered a head injury. Sadly, he never recovered. In the last hours of his life, his mom prayed desperately that God would save his life. But God said no. In her book, McClafferty describes her journey of seeking to understand and make sense of a horrible tragedy.

I met McClafferty at a writers' group meeting. She described the loss she'd experienced years prior and her confusion in wondering why, if God loved her, He hadn't cared enough to answer her prayers. Then, in a gentle tone, devoid of anger, she relayed how she had come to understand that she would never know why God hadn't chosen to save her son's life—and she expressed the peace that knowledge had given her.

In her book, McClafferty writes, "When I accepted the fact that I would never know, I was able to stop searching for the answer." She goes on to share a defining lesson in the last sentence of her book: "Sometimes, God doesn't change our circumstances, He changes us in our circumstances."

No one likes to endure hard seasons. But God often teaches us our greatest lessons in the hardest seasons. Will we allow Him to transform us? We don't have to waste our sorrows if we realize there is a greater purpose in what we go through.

"We shouldn't seek answers as much as we should seek God," says author and pastor Mark Batterson in *The Circle Maker*. "If you seek answers you won't find them, but if you seek God, the answers will find you." First Chronicles 22:19 says: "Now devote your heart and soul to seeking the LORD your God." A promise follows: "If you seek Him, He will be found by you" (1 Chronicles 28:9).

We can turn to God during times of deep trouble and confusion. We can pour out our hearts and ask Him hard questions about our blended family circumstances. "I don't want to waste my sorrows," a friend told me recently. "I'm asking God to help me find meaning in them."

Let's consider how God wants to change us instead of asking God to change our circumstances. The question becomes: "What do You want me to learn from this, God? I'm listening."

Heavenly Father, I don't want to waste my sorrows.
Teach me the lesson I need. I'm listening.

THOUGHT FOR THE DAY

God often teaches us the greatest
lessons during our hardest seasons.

70

Acceptance Is the Answer

Shall we accept good from God, and not trouble?

JOB 2:10

"Life is difficult. This is a great truth, one of the greatest truths. It is a great truth because once we truly see this truth, we transcend it. Once we truly know that life is difficult—once we truly understand and accept it—then life is no longer difficult. Because once it is accepted, the fact that life is difficult no longer matters."

Psychiatrist M. Scott Peck penned those words at the start of his book *The Road Less Traveled* forty years ago. The book made publishing history with more than ten years on the *New York Times* bestseller list and sales of more than seven million copies. Its simple but profound introduction offers a perspective worth pondering. Life *is* difficult. In John 16:33 Jesus tells us, "In this world you will have trouble. But take heart! I have overcome the world."

Acceptance provides the key to contentment and stability when in the midst of trouble. We find serenity when we stop fighting the challenges of life and accept adversity without grumbling.

What are you struggling to accept in your stepfamily? Disharmony? Lack of unity with your mate? Uncomfortable feelings? Loyalty bonds to the other home?

Acceptance recognizes the reality of our situation without demanding control of the variables. It allows us to quit insisting others change. We let go of our need to have everything our way. Acceptance doesn't mean we give up on our hopes and dreams, but it maintains a perspective of the present that offers a better understanding of the future.

We find a story of acceptance in the book of Job. The author introduces Job as a "blameless and upright" man (1:1). Job doesn't deserve the difficulties he's about to experience. Within the period of one day, messengers report to him the loss of his livestock, his servants, and his ten children. His response amazes me. "He fell to the ground in worship and said, 'Naked I came from my mother's womb, and naked I will depart. The LORD gave and the LORD has taken away; may the name of the LORD be praised.' In all this, Job did not sin by charging God with wrongdoing" (Job 1:20–22).

Job went straight to acceptance. I'm certain my response would have been different. Too often, I complain. I question. I search for answers.

Acceptance means we name our problems and embrace our struggles. We no longer insist on immediate solutions or demand complete understanding. Instead, we take our problems to God and lean on Him as we wait for answers. That's when we'll discover contentment amid our difficulties.

I don't like the struggles of stepfamily life, Lord.
I need Your help to accept them as part of my journey.

THOUGHT FOR THE DAY

Acceptance of our struggles brings serenity.

Coping with Grief: Reflect on It

1. Have you experienced joy and sorrow alongside each other? Do you feel guilty for being joyful while you feel sad? It's not uncommon for both to coexist in blended family life. Consider how you can allow them both to be part of your healing.

2. Children are also walking through grief. When we see misbehavior, consider their pain. Ask questions when they're mad or sad. Are they missing their other parent? Are they having a hard time with their new family? Being empathetic helps build relationships.

3. Do you struggle with accepting your circumstances? We won't always understand God's ways. Study the story of Job and how he found acceptance in adversity.

4. Unmet expectations often create grief in blended families. What white-picket-fence dreams have not come true for you? Ask for God's help to be a conqueror.

5. What lessons has God taught you during hard seasons?

THE POWER OF FUN
AND LAUGHTER

The Power of Play

A happy heart makes the face cheerful,
but heartache crushes the spirit.

PROVERBS 15:13

The school needs chaperones for the middle school field trip," my stepdaughter Adrianne said with a grin. "Do you want to go canoeing?"

"Canoeing? Seriously? Hmm." I wasn't sure if I was up for that.

But I agreed to go. And I'm thankful I did. Adrianne and I have fun memories of that day. We canoed together with a hundred other students, feeling confident in our ability—until we ran into another canoe. To our surprise, we both ended up in cold, murky water. We laughed and laughed while we tried to get back into the canoe. Although we can't account for exactly what happened, decades later, we have fond memories of that day.

If we take ourselves too seriously, life becomes dull. Try new adventures. Travel to unknown places. Laugh together. Create memories. Find things your family enjoys. We like to work puzzles and play board games. Some days, we enjoy a game of ping-pong or a round of basketball. The activity doesn't have to be extravagant or expensive. Conversation flows freely, and laughter breaks out easily in the midst of game-playing.

King Solomon gives advice about play. "So I recommend having fun, because there is nothing better for people in this world than to eat, drink, and enjoy life. That way they will experience some happiness along with all the hard work God gives them under the sun" (Ecclesiastes 8:15 NLT). We have plenty of hard work to do. Why not make time for fun and happiness, too?

My husband is a jokester who easily offers spontaneity and laughter for our family. In our early days, my serious nature tried to stifle his playful spirit. But I quickly learned the value of his sense of humor in the seriousness of stepfamily dynamics.

God has a sense of humor. We're made in His image—we don't have to carry around a serious demeanor all the time. Our stepchildren have been through divorce or the death of a parent and then remarriage. Maybe they only know the heaviness of loss and transition; pain and sadness have accompanied their days. They deserve an opportunity to experience laughter in their new family.

It's never too late to enjoy the power of play as a family. We might have to move outside our comfort zones, but relationship-building happens when we spend time with one another, creating memories of fun and laughter that stretch beyond the early years.

Heavenly Father, I often take life too seriously.
Show me how to experience fun and laughter with my family.

THOUGHT FOR THE DAY

Play offers the gift of laughter and
fun to stepfamily relationships.

72

Romancing Your Spouse

There is no fear in love. But perfect love drives
out fear .... We love because he first loved us.
1 JOHN 4:18–19

Romance provides a spark for marriage on cloudy days. But it easily gets pushed out if we're juggling overwhelming emotions or hard-to-navigate circumstances in our blended family.

God often reminds us of what's important to Him just when we need it. For two years now, my husband has worked out of state, almost 2000 miles away. He's gone for long stretches of time and is home about one week/per month. It's been a trying season, and at times, we find our relationship feels disconnected. But God spoke to me one morning about the value of romance in keeping a marriage alive during a distracted season. If we don't make an intentional effort, though, it might not happen.

If your stepfamily routine includes kids moving back and forth between homes, there's little time for more than a kiss some days in passing with your spouse. Romance requires planning, like the stepcouple I heard about who actually schedules sex—now that's intentional!

Romance could include early Saturday morning fun while the bedroom door is locked. Or a night away while the kids stay with grandma. It doesn't have to be elaborate. Get creative. Be intentional.

It's not likely you'll experience a romantic moment during blended family life every day. Or even every other day. But you can set up the opportunity with simple behaviors like taking time to compliment your spouse for their efforts in parenting your child or managing a stressful situation well with their former spouse. A grateful heart breeds contentment and can lead to romantic moments.

God must consider romance important to marriage since He dedicated an entire book of Scripture to it in Solomon's Song of Songs. Just as the beauty of a sunrise gives fresh energy to a mundane morning, romance can light up a distracted or overwhelmed marriage during a busy season.

Lord Jesus, thank You for your gift of love and romance.
Help me to prioritize that aspect of marriage
and to take time to romance my spouse.

THOUGHT FOR THE DAY

Romance provides a spark of sunshine
for marriage on cloudy days.

73

Your Unique Image

*My son, do not let wisdom and understanding out of
your sight, preserve sound judgment and discretion.*
PROVERBS 3:21

I gasped at the insurance rate quoted for our then-sixteen-year-old son. Nathan's a good kid. He's a calm driver with a clean record. But he has one very big issue that drives up his costs—he's sixteen! "We don't like to insure youthful drivers," the insurance agent said bluntly. *Really?* I thought. *That's obvious by the rate you quoted.*

Stereotyping. It happens all too frequently. Nathan had been stereotyped as a reckless male teenager, driven by testosterone that would result in major driving infractions with high dollar consequences. I hung up the phone and wanted to yell, "It's not fair! Stop the stereotyping!"

It happens in blended families, too. Have you felt it? We're quoted the statistics of blended families that fail and expect it will happen in our home, too. As a stepparent, you're not a "real" parent. Media contributes to the negative stereotyping with movies like *Cinderella*, *Snow White*, and *Stepmother*. We're given a bad rap before we even stroll into our stepchild's life. Stepmothers, especially, have to work twice as hard to overcome the "evil" stigma, the stereotyping.

It's not fair! How do we cope with it?

We can decide we won't follow the expectations presented, even when we're stereotyped a certain way. Our blended family doesn't have to experience failure. Nathan doesn't have to carry out the assumptions of the insurance company. We don't have to portray the picture that's painted of an evil stepparent.

Jesus didn't fit the stereotype of a king.

He was accused of hanging out with the wrong type of people. In Luke 5:30, the Pharisees asked Him, "Why do you eat and drink with tax collectors and sinners?"

He admitted to His reliance on God the Father. John 5:30 says, "By myself I can do nothing."

He served others in a humble fashion. In John 13, He washed His disciples' feet.

He was accused of being from the wrong place. We read in John 7:52, "Are you from Galilee, too? Look into it, and you will find that a prophet does not come out of Galilee."

In fact, Jesus refused to be defined by a stereotype. He created His own unique image—one that fit *His* identity as a king.

We have the same choice! We don't have to accept the definition projected by a stereotype. Regardless of what society expects, we can build blended family relationships that go the distance. We can create our own image of a stepparent—one who's loving, caring, and accepting of others. As we choose a different identity, we can pray for softened hearts of those around us to see us differently than a stereotypical image.

Dear Lord, thank You for my identity as a child of the King. Strengthen our blended family relationships and teach us to follow You as we guide our children.

THOUGHT FOR THE DAY

Don't allow stereotypes to drive your behavior.

74

Seize the Moment

Teach us to realize the brevity of life,
so that we may grow in wisdom.
PSALM 90:12 NLT

I gazed out the window, admiring the beauty of the snowfall. It was a rare occurrence in Louisiana, and I let myself slow down on a middle-of-the-week day. Instead of driving a carful of high school soccer players to an out-of-town game that was canceled, my son and I enjoyed a leisurely afternoon together. As the day wore on, a thought crept into my mind: *Will they be out of school again tomorrow? Can we gain another day at a slower pace?*

It's not easy to capture moments of leisure and enjoy meaningful time with our families. Sports, schoolwork, church events, community involvement, and other extracurricular activities compete for our time. But it's important to slow down. Time spent together bonds relationships.

Paul emphasizes the importance of how we spend our time: "Be very careful, then, how you live—not as unwise but as wise, making the most of every opportunity" (Ephesians 5:15–16). Living in the same house with our stepchildren doesn't automatically create integrated, thriving relationships. The atmosphere of our home and what we do together, "making the most of every opportunity," determines whether we encourage bonding.

Eating dinner together as a family and creating intentional togetherness takes time and effort. But it makes a difference. It might be easier to go to our bedroom and isolate ourselves from others, particularly after a hard day at work. It's okay to do that sometimes, but we can't do it every day if we're seeking to build relationships. We must be careful that we don't give into selfish desires that include only our needs.

"Whoever sows to please their flesh, from the flesh will reap destruction; whoever sows to please the Spirit, from the Spirit will reap eternal life" (Galatians 6:8).

We reap what we sow. And listen, dear one, here's the good part: "So let's not get tired of doing what is good. At just the right time we will reap a harvest of blessing if we don't give up" (Galatians 6:9 NLT). We're promised a harvest of blessing! I know it's hard to keep pouring into a relationship when you don't see results. It's hard to keep doing good to others when you don't know what kind of response you'll get in return. But you'll be blessed in the end, I promise. I can testify to it! On our blended family journey, I've experienced blessings too many to count. To God be the glory!

Heavenly Father, I don't always want to do good. I want to give into my selfish nature. Help me do my part to pursue healthy relationships with my stepfamily.

THOUGHT FOR THE DAY

Relationships bond as you spend time together.

75

Community Strengthens Us

Let us think of ways to motivate one another to acts of love
and good works. And let us not neglect our meeting together,
as some people do, but encourage one another,
especially now that the day of his return is drawing near.
HEBREWS 10:24–25 NLT

Our family visited Southern California's redwood forests recently. As I gazed at the magnificence of the trees, I wondered how the tall trunks could stay standing through destructive weather. *They must have incredibly deep roots,* I thought. But I was wrong. I learned that redwoods have shallow root systems, usually only five or six feet deep. It seems impossible that roots like that could hold up a 350-foot tree. However, while those roots don't go deep, they extend out as far as a hundred feet; they interlock and fuse together with the roots of their neighbors, creating a foundation strong enough to thrive in any weather. Redwoods grow taller than all other trees due to one main factor: community.

God created both nature and people in ways that require community to thrive. In stepfamilies, when we lock arms with those who understand our course, we gain encouragement, strength, and hope for our challenges. Relationships, particularly with fellow believers who offer listening ears and prayerful hearts, provide stability when circumstances threaten to knock us over. Our roots must extend wide to create the foundation we need for stormy seasons.

We see examples of community throughout Scripture. One of my favorites is the story of Mary and Elizabeth, found in Luke 1. Mary has just learned she is pregnant with Jesus by the power of the Holy Spirit. The angel Gabriel informs her, "So the holy one to be born will be called the Son of God." He gives few details and goes straight into a story regarding another miraculous pregnancy. "Even Elizabeth your relative is going to have a child in her old age, and she who was said to be unable to conceive is in her sixth month. For no word from God will ever fail" (Luke 1:36–37). Mary has just learned exciting but concerning news. What a beautiful offering, that God immediately informs her of someone in a similar situation. A rich friendship follows.

Mary leaves to visit Elizabeth in a town approximately eighty miles away, a long journey for a pregnant woman to travel by donkey. We aren't told why, but we can speculate that perhaps Mary knows Elizabeth will understand her perplexing situation. The two must have provided valuable support for one another as Mary stays with Elizabeth for three months.

God intends for us to walk alongside one another. More than just phone calls or text messages, true community includes physical presence. It fosters stability, strength, and hope. Extend a hand of encouragement to a fellow stepparent who's struggling. Befriend your coworker who needs a supportive ear with her difficult ex-spouse. You will both draw strength for the journey.

Thank You, Lord, for the beauty of relationships.
Help me do my part to create community with those around me.

THOUGHT FOR THE DAY

Community offers stability, strength, and hope.

76

Opening Your Heart to Extended Family

Dear friends, let us love one another, for love comes from God.
Everyone who loves has been born of God and knows God.

1 JOHN 4:7

"My first Christmas as a stepmom included many special moments," said my sister Jan. "But the most memorable centers around a simple gesture my mother-in-law did to help me feel included in the family."

Jan married Bob in late October and faced life in a new city with three stepchildren, ages eight, thirteen, and fifteen. Having never been married and without children of her own, she was excited about entering a family. But anxiety stirred with the upcoming holiday.

"I started unpacking Christmas boxes in Bob's basement one day," Jan said. "I found four homemade stockings for Bob and his three children that I could tell my mother-in-law had made years ago. Each beautifully worn and treasured stocking had stitching and decorations unique to the person. As I glanced at my overpriced, glitzy stocking purchased overseas, I couldn't shake the feeling of *I don't belong here—even my STOCKING looks different.*"

Determined to create special holiday memories, the newly married couple invited Bob's parents to their first Thanksgiving dinner as a family, knowing they would bring stability to their new season. "I was feeling weary, unequipped for my role, and out of place in my family, my home, and my new neighborhood," said Jan. "My mother-in-law's friendly hug at the door picked me up. As I welcomed her in, I noticed she carried a fabric stocking, along with bags of stickers, bells, tinsels, and letters of my name."

"I'd like to make you a stocking for your mantel," she said with a smile.

"I tried to hide the tears that rushed to my eyes," Jan remembered. "I was overwhelmed by her kindness—an unexpected gesture from a woman who barely knew me. I accepted her gracious invitation. After the Thanksgiving dinner, we sat down together to create my very special stocking."

Jan could have allowed her insecurities to keep her from building relationships with her new in-laws. Instead, she kept an open mind and a willing heart to receive their help and support. "God taught me to accept love from my new family members that year," Jan said. "I'm forever thankful. Now, my heart overflows with love for my mother-in-law each year as I hang my stocking. I'll always cherish the feeling of belonging she gave me during a vulnerable time of adjustment."

Dear Lord, I need Your help to build relationships with my extended family. Soften their hearts and mine to extend and receive love with one another.

THOUGHT FOR THE DAY

Building relationships with new in-laws offers belonging.

77

Encouraging a Stepgrandparent

Is not wisdom found among the aged?
Does not long life bring understanding?
JOB 12:12

For most of us, grandparents are fabulous! They are the adults who love us but don't have to discipline us. They relish the chance to spoil us because they don't have to take us home. And they carry a special place in our hearts.

Stepgrandparenting can be all that, too, if everyone agrees it can—and everyone wants it to happen. But that isn't always the case.

When Leslie married Barry, she noticed Barry's parents took little interest in her six-year-old son Noah. They had multiple grandchildren already and didn't seem interested in developing a relationship with Noah. Leslie's parents had passed away, and her heart ached as she thought about the lost opportunity Noah had to bond with a loving grandparent.

She asked Barry if he would consider talking with his parents about it. Did they recognize the impact they could have on Noah? Did they understand Noah's desire to have grandparents who loved and cared for him? Would they be willing to step out of their comfort zone and reach out to him?

Thankfully, Barry's parents were receptive. They didn't know about Noah's lack of grandparents in his life, and after a gentle nudge by their son, they opened their hearts to him.

Grandparents who sit on the sidelines miss out on a great opportunity and God-given responsibility to make a difference in their grandchildren's lives. We might need to help our parents understand that our children, both biological and stepchildren, need their influence, love, and guidance.

Scripture gives grandparents the responsibility of passing the baton of faith from generation to generation. "Only be careful, and watch yourselves closely so that you do not forget the things your eyes have seen or let them fade from your heart .... Teach them to your children and to their children after them" (Deuteronomy 4:9).

I'm thankful for the Christian influence, love, and kindness my parents showed to *all* their grandchildren. Although they have passed away, their legacy of spiritual influence and memories of meaningful time together will never be forgotten.

Heavenly Father, help our children's grandparents understand their spiritual influence and responsibility to pass the baton of faith as they stay connected in meaningful ways to our children. Bless their efforts.

THOUGHT FOR THE DAY

Grandparents carry a special influence on all their grandchildren, which we can encourage and empower.

78

Traditions Create Belonging

I praise you for remembering me
in everything and for holding to the
traditions just as I passed them on to you.

1 CORINTHIANS 11:2

Our heart-shaped waffle maker comes out of the pantry once a year—on Valentine's Day. The appliance barely does its job now and makes an annoying beep to signal the waffles are ready, but the tradition carries on. We make heart-shaped waffles with red food coloring the morning of February 14, whether it falls on a Monday or a Saturday.

Family traditions create identity for your family and help everyone feel connected. Unique experiences that happen year after year provide meaning and belonging. They don't have to be expensive or exaggerated. You can keep family traditions that still fit before your new family came together, but also consider new ones. Ask the kids for ideas. When our children were younger, we made paper chains to count down the days toward Christmas. We've also rung bells together for the Salvation Army. The girls and I like to bake special holiday desserts and distribute them to friends and neighbors.

Traditions allow for fun and laughter together, which helps protect a family against brokenness and conflict. Loyalty and commitment to one another form as the family looks forward and plans to gather for the same experiences year after year. When stepchildren travel between homes, traditions go smoother if we embrace flexibility. You might not experience smooth sailing in the beginning. If you try one that doesn't work well, find something different and begin again.

When our kids were younger, I desperately wanted them to enjoy picking out a live Christmas tree together—a happy childhood memory of my own. We'd plod around a tree lot, looking for just the right size and shape. Instead of happy dispositions, we experienced sour attitudes and sharp tongues toward one another in the middle of an exhausting season.

After several years of the same scene, my husband and I decided that tradition needed to end. To my chagrin, we bought an artificial tree. We started a new tradition of sorting out the limbs by their color coding and placing them in just the right spot to make our tree beautiful, despite the fact it was dead. I came to enjoy the new tradition that didn't include all the fussing.

Christians show praise and honor to the Lord Jesus Christ through traditions at Easter and Christmas. In the same way, we give honor to our family relationships as we create traditions on special days that help define our unique identity. Brainstorm a few ideas this year and find ways to have fun together in your blended family!

Help us, Lord, to find traditions that bring our relationships together with love and laughter and create belonging in our family.

THOUGHT FOR THE DAY

Traditions create identity for blended families
and offer each member a sense of belonging.

79

Lighten Up

Sing to him a new song; play skillfully, and shout for joy.
PSALM 33:3

I couldn't ignore the enticing aroma of Mexican food from a nearby restaurant as I walked into a cycling class at the gym. My friend joined me at the door and, with a mischievous grin, said, "Let's skip class and go eat chips and salsa. Wouldn't that be more fun?"

"Yes, it would!" I said. I entertained the thought for a moment before I replied. "But I won't enjoy my evening if I skip exercise today. What if we meet Friday for lunch and indulge in that food we're smelling?" She nodded in agreement as a smile spread across her face.

When we take time to enjoy activities that bring pleasure, we take the sting out of life's seriousness. Stepfamily life includes so much serious stuff like the labor of boundary-setting and raising up mature attitudes with our kids and stepkids. But it can also include going to the movies together or getting our nails painted. Everyone gains when we weave in fun activities with the mundane. Like my cycling decision, our laborious days can be coupled with leisure time.

After launching her stepson Braden to college recently, Katherine commented on her time as a stepmom during his adolescent years. "I always tried to remember that every stepparenting effort I made contributed to the maturing of a young man. My husband and I balanced the discipline of chores, homework, and respectful teaching with leisure time that included dinners out and vacations together. Informal time with Braden allowed me to stay connected, which in turn contributed to an attitude that more easily honored my requests regarding chores and respect."

I'm convinced Jesus had a sense of humor and enjoyed some light-hearted times with His disciples. Consider this word picture from His teaching that would likely bring a smile: "It is easier for a camel to go through the eye of a needle than for someone who is rich to enter the kingdom of God" (Mark 10:25). And His humorous questions like: "Which of you fathers, if your son asks for a fish, will give him a snake instead? Or if he asks for an egg, will give him a scorpion?" (Luke 11:11–12).

Although Jesus' work surrounding the cross, salvation, and resurrection was serious, He didn't neglect to use humor and light-heartedness in His ministry. We can do the same. We've been given the arduous task of connecting with our stepchildren and raising capable young adults with all our children, but we don't have to neglect fun and humor in the process. Find time for leisure. Share laughter and play. And watch your relationships blossom in the process.

Thank You, Lord, for Your example of humor and banter.
Help me to enjoy times of leisure and
playfulness with my stepfamily more often.

THOUGHT FOR THE DAY

We more easily develop connected relationships when we include time of leisure and playfulness in our home.

The Power of Fun and Laughter: Reflect on It

1. Do you consider how the power of fun and play can help build relationships? What have you done lately to capitalize on that?

2. What traditions has your family started that helped create belonging?

3. How can you encourage grandparents to be part of your children's lives? Do you need to give them a gentle nudge?

4. Do you look for common interests with your stepchildren? What can you do together that would help build a connected relationship?

5. Do you take life too seriously? Is it time to lighten up and create a family fun day that includes laughter and light-hearted time together?

BUILDING RELATIONSHIPS
THAT GO THE DISTANCE

80

Your Spouse or Your Children?

From [God's] glorious, unlimited resources,
he will empower you with inner strength through his Spirit.

EPHESIANS 3:16 NLT

"My daughter has been through so much since her dad passed away," Tiffany said. "I feel like I'm neglecting her when I spend time with my spouse. But Larry is also asking for my time and attention. How do I choose where to put my focus?"

The tug-of-war between our child and our spouse creates a common struggle for biological parents in blended families. I remember feeling it myself. My heart yearned to take my girls' pain away after my divorce. As a single mom, we spent days and nights together with my sole focus on them. But when I married again, my young daughters experienced another loss. My energy and attention were now going to my spouse for hours a day, leaving them to cope with their confusion and heartache without me.

As biological parents, we naturally feel pulled toward our children and often prioritize them over our spouse. We justify our behavior because of the hard road our children have already walked. But God's design for *every* family begins with the marriage, laying the foundation for the home. Children benefit from the stability and longevity it brings. Blended families are at a disadvantage here. Parent-child relationships predate the new marriage and have deeply rooted bonds. As a result, biological parents tend to prioritize their children, often creating strain and division in their marriage.

"Tiffany," I said. "Would you be willing to take a risk? Would you consider the benefits your daughter will gain as you prioritize your marriage and move toward your spouse? I'm not asking you to neglect your child, but rather help her understand that your marriage is important to you as well."

Risk-taking feels uncomfortable. But God gives us strength when we ask for His help. "From His glorious, unlimited resources, He will empower you with inner strength through His Spirit" (Ephesians 3:16 NLT). Inner strength gives us the courage to take a risk.

I remember when Randy helped his kids understand the value of our marriage. I was discouraged as a stepmom, feeling like an outsider in our home and wondering if my stepkids would ever accept me. One day, Randy brought us together and told his kids, "I love Gayla. She isn't going anywhere. I want us to figure out how to include her in our circle so she feels loved and accepted." I knew that was a risk for my husband, and it spoke volumes to my insecure heart. He prioritized our marriage that day.

Randy kept showing up in different ways to affirm his love for me in front of his kids. He didn't treat them differently or love them any less. He simply placed a high significance on our marriage in front of his kids.

Our spouse and our kids are both important. However, our *marriage* is more important to the foundation of the home, which, in turn, creates stability and security for our kids.

Dear Lord, I'm burdened by the road my kids have walked.
Too often, my focus is on them. Give me the
strength to prioritize my marriage as well.

THOUGHT FOR THE DAY

Balancing the tug-of-war between our kids and
our spouse brings stability to our home.

81

Self-Control Is the Right Choice

*[The grace of God] teaches us to say "No" to ungodliness
and worldly passions, and to live self-controlled,
upright, and godly lives in this present age.*

TITUS 2:12

As we read Scripture in our stepfamily class, I disagreed with one man's interpretation. "I look at the passage as a whole," he said. "I know I'm weak in some areas, but when I look at it altogether, I'm doing okay."

The passage was 2 Peter 1:5–7: "For this very reason, make every effort to add to your faith goodness; and to goodness, knowledge; and to knowledge, self-control; and to self-control, perseverance; and to perseverance, godliness; and to godliness, mutual affection; and to mutual affection, love." I knew the gentleman who spoke up was a great guy, but he struggled with self-control.

We don't get to consider how we're doing overall, nor can we choose the attributes that flow from us naturally. Perhaps "goodness" or "perseverance" reflect our everyday behavior, and we think we're doing okay. But we want to consider each attribute separately. They're *all* important. In stepfamily life, I would suggest that self-control is perhaps the most important. Without self-control, our lives breed destructive attitudes and actions, and we thwart healthy relationship-building.

Thoughts drive behavior. To control our actions, we first start with our thoughts. Philippians 4:8 says, "Finally, brothers and sisters, whatever is true, whatever is noble, whatever is right, whatever is pure, whatever is lovely, whatever is admirable—if anything is excellent or praiseworthy—think about such things." If we strive for positive attitudes and pure thoughts toward our stepchildren, our spouse, and even our ex-spouse, we will more easily maintain self-control.

But some days, we're rockin' along, minding our own business, when a grumpy stepdaughter throws a dagger our way. She's having a bad day, and we become the target of her anger. We become incensed, and we snarl right back.

Lysa TerKeurst offers advice for these moments in her book *Unglued*. "Feelings are indicators, not dictators, child. They can indicate where your heart is in the moment, but that doesn't mean they have the right to dictate your behavior and boss you around. You are more than the sum total of your feelings and perfectly capable of that little gift from Jesus called self-control!"

We don't have to be controlled by another's behavior. We get to *choose* how we respond! Instead of a snarky remark, perhaps we set a boundary—our stepdaughter goes to her room until her attitude improves.

TerKeurst has said, "I can face things that are out of my control and not act out of control." We'll naturally face difficult attitudes and behaviors with family. But we have a choice how we'll respond, with Jesus' help. Self-control is the right choice. Every time.

I need help with self-control, Lord. Some days, I just can't seem to control my tongue. Guard my thoughts and help me make better choices with my behavior. I want to be obedient to Your instructions.

THOUGHT FOR THE DAY

Self-control offers emotional safety in our relationships.

82

Opposing Standards Create Confusion

Why do you look at the speck of sawdust in your brother's
eye and pay no attention to the plank in your own eye?

MATTHEW 7:3

"I don't like the void of spiritual influence in their other home," a dad said to me. "We work hard to teach our kids to love the Lord and follow God's Word, but they have contrary standards at their mom's house."

Judging the standards in the other home because they're different from ours won't change anything. However, criticizing someone our child and stepchild love or the standards that person lives by will create barriers in your relationship with them. Scripture tells us, "Do not judge, or you too will be judged" (Matthew 7:1).

We can't control what takes place when our children move between homes. It's not uncommon for kids to experience different views of the Christian life. We can pray for godly influences, but they won't always be there. We can still trust that God will work out all things for His good (Romans 8:28).

When my girls were younger, I didn't like their exposure to a life marred by alcoholism at their dad's house. I wanted to protect them from his unhealthy choices and ongoing consequences. As the girls moved into their teenage years, they began to recognize the danger of drug and alcohol abuse. Without my prompting, conversation evolved about natural consequences regarding our choices. I'm thankful today to report the positive influence that observing their dad had on them to make right choices and escape the destruction of addiction.

Nothing speaks louder to our children and stepchildren than our own behavior. I learned recently of a dad who teaches his child to be honest at all times—except when his ex-spouse (the child's mother) is involved. The father regularly practices deception against his ex-spouse to extend visitation arrangements with the child or to manipulate the mother. How confusing it must be for that child to be disciplined for dishonesty by his dad, yet witness it practiced against his mother.

Opposing standards between our speech and our behavior create confusion for our children and stepchildren.

Poet Edgar Guest says it best:

I'd rather see a sermon than hear one any day;
I'd rather one should walk with me than merely tell the way.
The eye is a better pupil, more willing than the ear;
Fine counsel is confusing, but example is always clear.

Dear Lord, it's easier to look at the faults of others than consider my own. Show me my sinful ways. Give me the courage to face my judgmental attitudes and un-Christlike standards and the strength to change my behavior.

THOUGHT FOR THE DAY

Our behavior speaks louder than our words.

83

The Price of Forgiveness

Forgive as the Lord forgave you.

COLOSSIANS 3:13

After my first marriage ended, I held on to unforgiveness. I had been mistreated, and I justified my actions from a wounded soul. I was aware of what Scripture said, but I didn't want to consider how my unforgiveness contributed to my lack of peace and affected my daily walk with others and with the Lord.

Communication with my ex-husband was strained. Co-parenting seemed to be impossible—that is, until the day I realized how I contributed to the difficulty with my unforgiveness.

The same thing happens in stepfamilies. Wounded by hurtful words from our stepchild or misunderstood by our spouse, we hang onto unforgiveness, hindering our relationships. We feel justified because we've been wronged. As a result, tension coexists with every interaction in our home.

There's a price to pay for the choices we make. The price of unforgiveness is a burden of resentment, a poison of bitterness, and the heartache of strained relationships. The price of forgiveness is love, freedom, and peace.

Why do we choose poison over freedom? Because when we've been wronged, forgiveness is hard. It doesn't happen naturally. But when we seek the Lord's help and intentionally make the choice to go against our human nature, we find the ability to forgive.

Christ paid a huge price so we could experience forgiveness. His death on the cross is a powerful reminder of the sacrifice He offered us. But even Christ struggled with doing what the Father asked of Him. Matthew 26:39 says, "Going a little farther, He fell with His face to the ground and prayed, 'My Father, if it is possible, may this cup be taken from me. Yet not as I will, but as you will.'"

Some days, we'd rather say, "Not Your will, but mine." My will includes justifying my hurt and wallowing in my misery. My will seeks to take care of myself instead of considering others' needs. Unfortunately, following my own will also leads to a life of heartache and disappointment.

My pastor's words recently spoke to my heart: "Unforgiveness is demanding that other people be perfect, and that's a standard you can't meet!" If I fail to forgive my stepchildren for an imperfect action, I'm expecting they'll never have to forgive me for a wrong. I make imperfect choices every day.

Why, then, do I hold onto unforgiveness?

Forgiveness provides the key to unlocking tension in stepfamily relationships. We're called to forgive, even when it's not our fault. It's not easy, but when we choose to be obedient to God's call, we experience peace and joy in our relationships.

Thank You, Lord, for always forgiving me,
although I don't deserve it. Help me offer
forgiveness to others, even on days I don't feel like it.

— THOUGHT FOR THE DAY —

There's a price to pay for the choices we make.

84

Maturity Required

By this everyone will know that you are my disciples, if you love one another.

JOHN 13:35

In my mom's last year with Alzheimer's, she rarely knew me or my sisters. At times, my immature self would get irritated with her confused look, and I wanted to yell, "How can you not know me? I've been your daughter for fifty-five years!" But my mature self always stepped in and took over. I reminded Mom—again—who I was, wrapped my arms around her, and asked what I could do to help. Even when I didn't feel like it, I knew it was the right choice.

We have opportunities every day to make mature or immature choices in our stepfamily relationships. Sometimes we have a split second to consider how we'll respond. It might require a quick prayer to ask for God's help first. But even when we don't feel like it, a mature response is the right choice, every time.

In his book *Emotionally Healthy Spirituality*, Peter Scazzero says, "It is impossible to be spiritually mature while remaining emotionally immature." Too often, we check off the boxes of spirituality that make us feel we're living a good Christian life. We read our Bible, help with mission work, go to church, and perhaps even sing in the choir. But if someone followed us around and watched how we treated others in our own family, emotional maturity wouldn't match the spiritual maturity we claim through our Christian work.

I'm not saying it's easy. Responding in kindness when your stepchild snarls at you doesn't come naturally. Self-control during a heated argument takes intentional effort. Offering a smile when you want to throw out a scowl takes a moment of self-reflection. God walks with us. Ask for His help.

It's easier to read the Bible than follow its directives. We'll gain more joy from singing in the choir than helping a grumpy stepchild with his homework. We would rather volunteer at the shelter than work through the conflict in our home. But we're not called to only carry out acts of spiritual maturity. We're also called to walk in emotional maturity with those around us.

A heart that runs after God more easily spills over with emotional maturity. We find the perfect model in Scripture. Luke 5:16 says, "But Jesus often withdrew to lonely places and prayed."

When we prioritize time for *being* with God, we're better at *doing* what God calls us to do.

Heavenly Father, in my life yoked to busyness, I don't include enough time with You. Show me the steps I need to take to walk in emotional and spiritual maturity.

THOUGHT FOR THE DAY

Spiritual and emotional maturity paves a road for loving stepfamily relationships.

85

The Tug-of-Loyalty Conflict

Above all, clothe yourselves with love,
which binds us all together in perfect harmony.

COLOSSIANS 3:14 NLT

"The senior sports banquet was a disaster," Lizzy said with a disgusted look. "I wanted a picture of my stepson Jack and his dad together, but he wouldn't leave his mom's side. I guess he felt sorry for her because she was by herself. When I finally asked for a picture of just the two of them, Jack got mad. What did I do wrong?"

"I know you had good intentions," I said. "But it sounds like Jack's loyalty radar was up. With his new stepmom making requests that excluded his mom, he felt protective of her."

Loyalty conflict presents a common hurdle in blended families. Children feel conflicted when they're asked to pick sides or exclude one parent over another. A winner and a loser emerge—and the child feels guilty for their choice.

I recently took on the new role of mother-in-law. I've considered how it would feel if my daughter were forced to take sides between her husband and me. If I compete with her husband and make demands for love and attention that exclude him, she'll pull away from me and move toward him. She loves us both; she shouldn't have to choose between us.

It's no different with our children and stepchildren. When they get caught in the middle between people they love, they'll pull away. If we judge or criticize their other parent, then we push children into picking sides. Competition breeds jealousy and resentment.

There's enough love to go around.

A biological parent in the other home can feel threatened by a stepparent, but we can avoid that by letting them know we have no intention of taking their place.

It's important we recognize their unique role as a parent. We can express our desire to come alongside, to love and support their child without impeding their space.

Colossians 3:12 teaches us to "clothe yourselves with compassion, kindness, humility, gentleness and patience." When we consider the tug of loyalty children experience, we can more easily show them compassion and kindness. Humility in our interactions with those inside and outside our stepfamily circle lessens the urge to compete with one another.

There's an African proverb that says, "When the music changes, so does the dance." Loyalty conflict often shows up unannounced and changes the music for our stepchildren. We honor their feelings and promote relationship-building when we change our dance to reflect their changing music.

Heavenly Father, give me understanding when my stepchildren experience loyalty conflict; help me do my part to assuage it.

THOUGHT FOR THE DAY

We show honor to children when we allow
an allegiance to both their parents.

86

Behavior That Pleases God

The Lord detests the way of the wicked,
but he loves those who pursue righteousness.

PROVERBS 15:9

"Adversity doesn't build character; it reveals it." These words by James Lane Allen circled in my thoughts. What kind of character was being revealed by the challenge I faced? Was I following John 3:30 that says: "He must become greater; I must become less"? What does that really mean?

The story of Joseph in Genesis 37 gives us a glimpse. Joseph was born into a blended family, the youngest of twelve sons. Jacob "loved Joseph more than any of his other sons, because he had been born to him in his old age" (37:3). Joseph's brothers knew he was the favorite, and they hated him. One day, they threw him into a pit to die. Feeling guilty because he was their brother, however, they retrieved him and instead sold him into slavery for a meager price. For thirteen years, Joseph experienced humiliation, suffering, and intense loneliness, though he had done nothing wrong.

Joseph met his adversity with courage, determined to seek after God's calling for his life even when he didn't understand his circumstances. His absence of grumbling through suffering revealed his unwavering trust in God. He allowed God's presence to guide him, refusing to let sin take hold in any way with his attitude or his behavior—a testimony that revealed more of God and less of self.

After years of adversity, God rewarded Joseph for his faithful walk. Genesis 39:23 says, "The Lord was with Joseph and gave him success in whatever he did."

What about our adversity in stepfamily life? What would it look like to have less of self and more of God? Here are a few examples:

- A humble approach to our stepchild's behavior problem, instead of prideful words that insist we know best.
- A willing heart to take extra steps toward building healthy relationships.
- Kind words to our stepchild without expecting of the same behavior in return.
- A neutral response, instead of a nasty one, when our spouse's ex changes the visitation schedule ... again.
- Behavior that shows love and understanding to our spouse, regardless of the behavior shown to us.

We need God's help to display "less of self" in our attitudes and actions. It takes intentional effort and a mind set on His will, not our sinful nature. But when you commit to follow God's ways, your plans will succeed.

Heavenly Father, I want my character to reveal more of You. Help me push aside my selfish ways and allow Your Spirit to guide my behavior.

THOUGHT FOR THE DAY

We reveal a character that pleases God when we model less of self and more of Him.

87

Humility Brings Harmony

Be completely humble and gentle; be patient,
bearing with one another in love.

EPHESIANS 4:2

In a conversation with our teenage son, I realized I'd offended him when I texted bluntly, "I need you to be more responsible next time." He'd asked for my help to look for something he thought he'd left at home but actually found in his athletic bag later. He didn't include a "please" or a "thank you" and assumed I'd drop what I was doing and help. As a result, my response wasn't as kind as it could have been.

I had several hours to let my emotions settle and think how I would respond that afternoon. When Nathan came in, he walked past me without saying a word.

"I'm sorry I implied you're not responsible," I said. "You *are* responsible. But next time you need help, I'd like a more courteous request with manners, please."

Humility shows honor to the person with whom we're interacting. Humble responses take effort, but they encourage relationship-building and positive communication. We find examples of humility throughout Scripture. The night of the Passover meal presents one unmatched.

Jesus made plans to celebrate the Passover with His disciples. He knew it would be His last meal with them, and He would soon be crucified. Before the meal began, He got a towel and a basin to wash the disciples' feet—feet that must have been dirty and smelly. And though He knew Judas Iscariot would later betray Him, that didn't change His behavior. Jesus took the position of a lowly servant and washed even the feet of the enemy. It's a display of humility that's hard to comprehend.

In our blended family homes, humility is the soil that cultivates harmony. Romans 12:16 says: "Live in harmony with one another. Do not be proud, but be willing to associate with people of low position. Do not be conceited."

Blessings follow when we honor one another in humility.

We demonstrate humility through our behavior, which includes our listening. Especially with our stepchildren, when we take extra steps to hear more than just their words, understanding follows. As we humbly—and without judgment—observe their mannerisms, their facial expressions, and their grunts and pauses, we begin to understand their feelings and motives.

God honors the humble and humbles the proud. Which will you choose?

Dear Lord, I want the blessings that humility offers. Show me how to serve and honor others in humility with my speech and my behavior. Help me follow Your model.

THOUGHT FOR THE DAY

Humility is the soil that cultivates harmony.

88

Coping with Difficult People

Brothers and sisters, if someone is caught in a sin,
you who live by the Spirit should restore that person gently.
But watch yourselves, or you also may be tempted.

GALATIANS 6:1

Our son, Nathan, suffers from severe allergies and asthma. During the spring and summer, he can seldom go outdoors without feeling the effects of heightened pollen counts and other allergens. In fact, his pediatrician told us we couldn't even leave the windows open during peak periods. He suffers more when the allergens invade our home.

Pollen in our home acts as a poison for Nathan, and consequences of illness follow. In the same way, difficult people in our lives can serve as poison that infiltrates our being, leaving behind a wake of resentment. We can't leave the windows of our soul open for offensive people to injure us.

My friend Jessica is a peacekeeper. She avoids conflict with her defiant stepdaughter until she can no longer stand it. Then she explodes. Her husband wants to help, but she pushes him aside in the midst of her anger and character assassination of her stepdaughter. Jessica doesn't understand how to have healthy conflict that will move toward reconciliation.

When we gently and lovingly confront another's behavior—if we act as peace*makers* instead of peace*keepers*—we are more likely to find a resolution. A peacemaker gets to the root and works through conflict in a calm and intentional manner.

In their book *Peacemaking Women,* Tara Barthel and Judy Dabler talk about the need to confront:

As difficult as it is, sometimes we are called to go humbly to the people who have wronged us in order to help them to understand better how they have contributed to our conflicts. Of course, when appropriate, we should be quick to overlook (Proverbs 19:11), and we must always first confess our own sins (Matthew 7:5). But if after we have confessed our own sins we cannot overlook the offense, we are called to help the person who has offended us by gently restoring her (Galatians 6:1) and helping her remove the speck from her eye (Matthew 7:5).

First, we consider our responsibility to overlook an offense and confess our own sin, if that's part of the conflict. Then, when necessary, we humbly confront. In stepfamily homes, there is an additional step. When confronting a difficult stepchild, have your spouse at your side. Stepchildren accept correction better when the biological parent takes part in difficult conversations.

Heavenly Father, I don't always know when to confront a difficult person. Give me wisdom and discernment on how to handle the conflict I experience in my home.

THOUGHT FOR THE DAY

A peacemaker wisely and lovingly confronts offensive people when necessary.

89

The Power of Boundaries

Live in harmony with one another.

ROMANS 12:16

Sitting across the table from a stepmom in tears, I suspected a boundary problem. I listened to Jenna describe her stepson's fits of rage and disrespectful language toward her and her husband. At seventeen, Josh controlled their home. But Jenna didn't know what to do.

"How does your husband respond to his son's actions?" I asked.

"It becomes a yelling match to see who can get in the last word," Jenna responded. "I often leave the house and take our daughter with me. I can't stand to watch it unravel. But the worst is when my husband isn't home, and Josh targets me. His outbursts are becoming increasingly more violent, and I'm scared to confront him—he's bigger and stronger than I am."

We teach our children how to treat others through how we respond to their behavior. When we respond to yelling with more yelling, that behavior becomes acceptable. Without healthy boundaries, we set ourselves up for embittered relationships and create self-centered adults in the process.

In their book *Boundaries*, Drs. Henry Cloud and John Townsend say it this way: "Boundaries help us keep the good in and the bad out. We need to keep things that will nurture us inside our fences and keep things that will harm us outside."

Boundary-setting shows up in the first book of the Bible. God clearly communicates His expectations to Adam: "You are free to eat from any tree in the garden; but you must not eat from the tree of the knowledge of good and evil, for when you eat of it, you will surely die" (Genesis 2:16–17). When Adam breaches those boundaries, consequences follow.

Jenna and her husband will have to set firm boundaries with Josh, along with consequences. Without them, he will continue to control their home.

Too often, in blended family homes, we parent out of guilt. Because our children and stepchildren have been through divorce or the death of a parent and a new family structure, we let our emotions prevent wise parenting decisions. We don't follow the pattern we find in Scripture.

When we fail to set boundaries, we encourage problems for our children in adulthood. If Josh doesn't change his ways, his lack of anger management will haunt him as an adult in employment opportunities and future relationships.

Boundary-setting is not black and white. God will provide the wisdom and discernment we need if we ask. "If any of you lacks wisdom, you should ask God, who gives generously to all without finding fault, and it will be given to you" (James 1:5).

Dear Lord, thank You for Your example of boundary-setting in the Garden of Eden. Help me and my spouse find unity in our decisions and give us wisdom and courage to create healthy boundaries in our home.

THOUGHT FOR THE DAY

Thriving relationships require healthy boundaries.

90

Sweet Talk Binds Relationships

Kind words are like honey—sweet to
the soul and healthy for the body.

PROVERBS 16:24 NLT

I wish I could say that kind and gentle words roll off my tongue naturally and with little effort—that I never offend others with what I say. Sadly, I can't. I tend to be a get-to-the-point conversation maker who can throw out direct and insensitive comments, particularly during a heated exchange. My husband says I insist on having the last word during an argument. It's not a flattering attribute.

I've worked hard to change. I recognize that my direct communication style can be misunderstood by others. If I'm passionate about an issue, I've learned to proceed cautiously with my words. Pausing before I speak results in fewer apologies later.

Kindness makes a big difference. When we mess up, apologies matter. As stepparents, it takes intentional effort on our part to be loved and accepted by our stepchildren. Biological children have a natural love for their parents, even when a parent fails. It's rarely the same with stepchildren.

We connect over time as we offer kind and loving words. Particularly when our stepchildren feel pulled by a string—loving us feels disloyal to their biological parent—we must go the extra mile to offer support and encouragement. We can find opportunities to be the "good guy" with a simple compliment or gesture of help.

There's a difference between *kindness* and *niceness*. We're nice to someone when we ask if they're hurt. We're kind when we offer a Band-Aid. Kindness is from the heart—it goes deeper than polite words. Actions must follow our words. We don't talk about acts of niceness; we talk about acts of kindness.

Too often, we're nice but not kind. We say nice things, but we don't really care about the person. We use polite language without sincerity. Sure, nice words sound good. But they won't reach into the heart and connect. Kindness will.

When we read about kindness in Scripture, it's often paired with traits such as compassion, goodness, gentleness, and grace.

- "Clothe yourselves with compassion, kindness, humility, gentleness and patience" (Colossians 3:12).
- "Be kind and compassionate to one another, forgiving each other, just as in Christ God forgave you" (Ephesians 4:32).
- "But the fruit of the Spirit is love, joy, peace, forbearance, kindness, goodness, faithfulness, gentleness and self-control" (Galatians 5:22–23).

Kindness speaks a unique language that tells people they matter. To your step-child, it says, "You're important." To your spouse, it says, "I love you." To your ex-spouse, it says, "You deserve forgiveness."

Kindness counts!

Heavenly Father, it's easy to be nice but hard to be kind.
Give me courage and motivation to offer kindness,
regardless of how others respond.

THOUGHT FOR THE DAY

Kindness counts!

Building Relationships That Go the Distance: Reflect on It

1. As a biological parent, it's not uncommon to struggle with the tug-of-war between your spouse and your children. But it's important to give significance to your marriage as the foundation of the home. What action can you take today that shows your spouse they're important to you? Consider how to prioritize your marriage for a healthy home.

2. Joseph was born into a blended family and faced adversity for many years. God eventually rewarded his faithful walk in huge ways. Read Joseph's story in Genesis 37–50 and consider how he walked in righteousness even when others were mistreating him and the blessings he received in the end.

3. Do your stepchildren experience loyalty conflict between you and their biological parent in the other home? What action will you take to help them?

4. Kindness helps build relationships that go the distance. What act of kindness will you extend today to someone in your family?

5. Do you parent out of guilt because of the road that your children have walked? Should you consider healthy boundary-setting with unacceptable behavior? To learn more about boundaries, read *Boundaries with Kids* or *Boundaries* by Drs. Henry Cloud and John Townsend.

GOD'S REDEEMING POWER

Live Fearlessly

For God has not given us a spirit of fear and timidity,
but of power, love, and self-discipline.

2 TIMOTHY 1:7 NLT

Her swollen eyes revealed her pain. Tears began as the stepmom spoke: "Why is this so hard? My stepchildren are adults. We rarely see them, but when we do, hurtful words fly."

Whether stepchildren are young or old, stepfamily adjustments exist. Unhealed wounds of the past can drive stepchildren to intimidate and alienate a stepparent from the family circle. The adage "Hurt people hurt people" rang true for this mom's stepdaughter.

It takes a spirit "of power and of love" from God to reach out after hurtful daggers have been thrown our way. Fear cripples our ability to respond. But this stepmom chose to continue to reach out with compassion. Eventually, her adult stepdaughter accepted her gestures of love.

In my own stepfamily, loving relationships didn't develop quickly. In our early years, we often took two steps forward and ten steps backward. I remember wanting to quit. But when I claimed the spirit of power that God offered, I gained confidence in my stepmom role.

Elisabeth Elliot, wife of martyred missionary Jim Elliot, stands out as a woman of rare courage. Elliot's husband was brutally killed while bringing Christianity to a primitive tribe in the jungles of Ecuador. She later determined the only way to find closure from her husband's death (and the deaths of four other missionaries killed by natives) was to live among the murderers with her young daughter, in hopes of bringing Jesus to them.

What an incredible feat! Elliot couldn't have walked into such an environment without supernatural love and power. She plunged ahead into the role she believed God had called her to, knowing the danger. For two years, accompanied by her daughter, she ministered to the tribe members who had left her widowed.

I doubt few of us will be called to model such courage in our day-to-day lives. But like Elliot, we can walk fearlessly into the role God has called us to—even when it's hard—if we ask Him to guide our steps and we show the spirit of love and power He has given us.

The stepparent journey includes days of bumpy roads and overwhelming emotions. But God provides the tools we need for a sure and steady walk. "The secret," Elisabeth Elliot says, "is Christ in me—not me in a different set of circumstances."

Heavenly Father, I want to live fearlessly in my stepparenting role, but I can't do it alone. I claim Your promise today that I've been given a spirit of power.

THOUGHT FOR THE DAY

With God's power, we are not without hope.

Partner with God

For the foolishness of God is wiser than human wisdom,
and the weakness of God is stronger than human strength.

1 CORINTHIANS 1:25

As I looked at the bookshelf bursting with parenting and stepparenting books, I thought, *How often do I turn to a book instead of seeking the Source with the best answer?*

Don't get me wrong—I love books. Books can give us tools to make our blended family journey go smoother. But they can't help with every issue stepfamilies face. A one-size-fits-all solution doesn't exist.

After my stepchildren lost their mom to cancer, we went through turbulent waters. Adrianne had just started college, and we didn't expect her to relocate from her mom and stepdad's house. But we did plan to move Payton into our home a few weeks after the funeral. You can imagine our surprise when, one Sunday afternoon, Randy opened the door to a sheriff delivering custody papers. Payton's stepdad had filed for custody!

After we absorbed the initial shock, we questioned what steps to take next. We sought an attorney to help, but we found ourselves asking questions that few had faced before. We turned to the one Source we knew could provide the answer.

Following the first court hearing, Randy and I had no peace about fighting the custody battle. We had three children in our home who would be heavily impacted by CPS interrogation, back-and-forth court hearings in another state, ongoing legal expenses, and two stressed-out parents. We chose to leave Payton where he was to grieve the loss of his mom with his stepdad, older sister, and half-brother. It was a tough decision, but we sensed the Lord's direction as the right choice at the time.

The series of events the next year surprised us. Nine months after his mom passed away, Payton willingly chose to move to our home without tension or animosity. We realized that after his much-needed time to grieve the loss with other family members going through the same emotions, he was now ready to come back to our home. God's guidance that year had helped us make a difficult choice.

Too often, we neglect to turn to God with our stepfamily challenges. We call a friend, pick up a book, go to the internet, or trust our own judgment. However, "Only God can give you the wisdom you need," says Stormie Omartian in *The Power of Praying for Your Adult Children.* "And He will give it to you when you ask for it. ... Prayer is not telling God what to do. Prayer is partnering with God to see that His will is done."

Thank You, Lord, for Your guiding hand.
Give me wisdom for our blended family journey.
I want to partner with You today and every day.

THOUGHT FOR THE DAY

There's power in prayer!

93

The Promise of God's Power

He said to me, "My grace is sufficient for you, for my power is made
perfect in weakness." Therefore I will boast all the more gladly
about my weaknesses, so that Christ's power may rest on me.

2 CORINTHIANS 12:9

I hadn't seen Margaret in years. After attending our stepfamily class at church, her family moved, and we lost contact. I knew the relationship with her stepdaughter had been strained, and I wasn't sure if they would ever connect. She found me on Facebook recently and sent a message that brought tears to my eyes, "Thank you for encouraging me to stay the course, even when it was hard. God restored the relationship with my stepdaughter. His strength sustained me during a hard season. Now, as a young adult, she lives close by, and we spend time together regularly. Praise God!"

Stepparenting brings many things. It can bring joy, hardship, or everything in between. We aren't promised a perfect life; we can expect difficult times along with the good. God offers us His strength. His power can provide all we need to navigate the stepfamily journey, but we have to ask for it to be manifested in our lives.

Perhaps you've asked God to remove the challenges and uncomfortable feelings you face in stepfamily life. That would be easier. But like Margaret's situation, we often have to wade through our difficulties, asking for God's help along the way. Can we respond as Paul did? "Therefore I will boast all the more gladly about my weaknesses, so that Christ's power may rest on me."

In 2 Corinthians 12:7, Paul says, "I was given a thorn in my flesh." Scripture doesn't tell us what his thorn is, but Paul begs the Lord to take it away. Instead, he's told, "My grace is sufficient for you" (12:9).

God's power provides all we need. When we feel inadequate, His power offers peace. When our circumstances appear bleak, He offers hope. When our relationships feel out of balance, God's power can bring harmony.

We don't have to live by how we feel; we can live by what we know. God's power raised Jesus Christ from the dead. He can bring restoration and healing to our homes. His grace is sufficient.

Thank You, Lord, for the promise of Your power to rest on me during times of weakness. Today, I ask that You demonstrate the magnificence of Your power and bring healing and redemption to struggling relationships. I love you, Lord and trust Your promises.

THOUGHT FOR THE DAY

God's power provides all we need.

94

Loving a Prodigal

While he was still a long way off, his father saw him and
was filled with compassion for him; he ran to his son,
threw his arms around him and kissed him.

LUKE 15:20

She felt the knot in her stomach tighten as the phone rang, knowing her husband was visiting his son in prison. Familiar feelings of anger, fear, and shame flooded her heart. *How did we get here?* she thought.

My stepmom friend Nancy had never been married nor had children of her own. She'd entered stepfamily life full of excitement and hope. Her expectations quickly turned to disillusionment, however, when they returned from their honeymoon. Her stepson had entered their home without permission and hosted a raucous party for his teenage friends. Her idyllic world took a dramatic turn as she uncovered empty beer cans and listened to her neighbor's reports of disturbance.

Nancy was raised in a safe and loving Christian home where respect for authority laid a foundation for family stability. She believed God had brought her and her husband together to redeem a broken family. Instead, their home became a hotbed of rebellion as her stepson defied their values and rules. But she never quit trusting God for brighter days and renewed relationships. Even in the darkness, Nancy drew strength from knowing God saw her prodigal stepson as His beloved child and longed to be in relationship with him. She focused on God's Word to find hope for her discouragement:

- "Don't be afraid, I've redeemed you. I've called your name. You're mine. When you're in over your head, I'll be there with you. When you're in rough waters, you will not go down" (Isaiah 43:1–4 MSG).

- "Count on it—there's more joy in heaven over one sinner's rescued life than over ninety-nine good people in no need of rescue" (Luke 15:7 MSG).

Loving a prodigal requires radical compassion that doesn't fixate on behavior. Instead, it pursues the heart. The chains of sin are strong, but God still redeems the lost. After years of broken promises, failed drug recovery programs, and even a year in prison, Nancy's stepson now works in another state and lives on his own. God is healing broken relationships, and their family is making new memories built on forgiveness and trust for the road ahead.

There is hope for anyone whose children are in the far country. God hears your prayers. You can trust Him to faithfully pursue the wandering heart of your prodigal with unfailing compassion and a never-ending love.

Dear Lord, help me keep my eyes on You when I become weary of loving my rebellious stepchild. Please expose any unforgiveness toward my prodigal. Give me the courage to persevere with renewed hope.

THOUGHT FOR THE DAY

Be faithful to pray for your prodigal,
then trust God for the outcome.

95

God's Tender Mercies

Jesus looked at them and said,
"With man this is impossible,
but with God all things are possible."

MATTHEW 19:26

Ginger Gilbert Ravella never expected the dramatic turn her life would take one fateful day. She was the mother of five young children when she lost her husband, Major Troy Gilbert, a USAF F-16 fighter pilot, in combat on November 27, 2006. Gilbert's heroic mission to save fellow soldiers in trouble cost him his life in a desert twenty miles outside of Baghdad. Al-Qaeda fighters immediately captured his body, rolled it in a carpet, and stashed it away. It would not be found for a long, long time. But Ginger never quit asking God for what seemed impossible—that Troy's body would come home.

Ginger's story, as told in her inspirational memoir, *Hope Found,* reveals a courage and a steadfast character found only through hope in Christ. Her unwavering faith carried her through a long, dark season as she mourned the death of her husband and walked an unwanted road as a single mom. Later, she remarried and took on the role of stepmom to her husband's two sons, who'd lost their mom to breast cancer.

Navigating loss and hardship was only part of her story. She refused to abandon the relentless search for Troy's stolen body. Although enough of his remains were discovered to support DNA identification, Ginger longed for his body to be returned. She never quit asking God for a miracle.

Ten years later, she received a call she didn't know would ever come. "They've found Troy," said Air Force General Robin Rand.

Ginger credits God's tender mercies for the final discovery of Troy's body. "The unit that recovered Troy's remains was the same unit that Troy saved all those years ago. God Himself gave us this final piece of closure. It was grace and mercy beyond understanding," she says.

"Because of the LORD's great love we are not consumed, for His compassions never fail" (Lamentations 3:22). God's tender mercies are new every morning.

What mountain do you face today in your stepfamily? A difficult ex-spouse who creates havoc in your home? A surly teenager who refuses to accept you into her life? A financial concern you don't have an answer for?

God still moves mountains. We don't have to walk alone. He will guide our steps, provide wisdom and understanding, and offer comfort through our hardships. But we must ask Him. Are you willing to seek His counsel?

Heavenly Father, I face mountains today I can't move.
I want to trust that You can. Give me unwavering faith
in my struggles and guide my steps to follow Your plan.

THOUGHT FOR THE DAY

God still moves mountains.

96

Great Is Thy Faithfulness

His unfailing love for us is powerful;
the LORD's faithfulness endures forever.
Praise the LORD!

PSALM 117:2 NLT

Many years ago, I was asked to head up a ministry team for a cause close to my heart. I had few concerns; it was a good thing, as I wholeheartedly believed (and still believe today) in its mission. But not long into the position, I felt drained by relationship issues. Conflict, lack of dedication by some, and insecurities by others began to create barriers within the core team. I didn't feel my voice as a leader was being heard, and I began to question my decision to move forward with the group.

As I prayed about my next steps one morning, I sensed a prompting in my spirit to stay the course. It was as if God said, "Continue to lead the group regardless of how others respond. Your job for now is to lead. I'll take care of the rest."

I wrestled with that choice but began to pray for unity and softened hearts with relationships on our team. I did my part to make amends for ways I might have offended others, and I worked hard to lead with a humble and considerate spirit. I asked God to show His faithfulness in our team relationships.

Within a few short days, I watched the conflict I was burdened by resolve. The team began to make strides on an event that had stagnated due to differing opinions. And once again, I gained confidence in the direction our ministry was headed.

I don't take credit for the change. When we can't, God can. Similarly, we can expect the same thing in our blended family relationships.

Perhaps you and your spouse struggle to find unity when parenting. Maybe you're not given the respect you deserve for the stepparent role you're called to. Or your ex-spouse makes constant changes to the visitation schedule, creating havoc in your home.

Pray for unity in your family and softened hearts toward one another. Do your part to make amends in areas that might have brought offense. Carry a humble and considerate spirit with others. And expect God's faithfulness to show up in your relationships.

You don't have to carry your burdens alone. Take them to Jesus. He can help!

Forgive me, Lord, when I try to work out my stepfamily struggles on my own. I know Your ways are better than mine. I'm asking for Your help to build and maintain healthy relationships and harmony in our home. Thank You for Your faithfulness.

THOUGHT FOR THE DAY

When we can't, God can.

97

Prayer Strengthens Us

Do not fear, for I am with you; do not be dismayed, for I am your God. I will
strengthen you and help you; I will uphold you with my righteous right hand.

ISAIAH 41:10

Words tumbled out from my friend, a new stepmom. "My stepson didn't acknowledge me at his graduation. When he walked over to give his dad a hug, he didn't even look at me." She dug for a tissue as she spoke of the awkwardness of the moment with her stepson's mom a few feet away. The pull of loyalty toward his mother resulted in rejection toward his stepmom. It's an unfair circumstance almost every stepparent experiences.

How do you cope? As stepparents, we're forced to walk through rejection, grief, and disappointment, particularly in the early years. We can't control our stepchildren's behavior toward us. But we have the power of prayer and confidence from God's promises to sustain us.

At 120 years old, Moses told the people of Israel, "I am no longer able to lead you" (Deuteronomy 31:2). He summoned Joshua and passed the baton to him to carry out the mission of crossing the Jordan into the promised land. He said to Joshua, "The LORD Himself goes before you and will be with you; He will never leave you nor forsake you. Do not be afraid; do not be discouraged" (31:8).

Joshua walked confidently with the Lord—surrendered to His plan and purposes. He found the courage to face his fears and strength to overcome hardship. We read about the beautiful reward God offered Joshua for his faithfulness. He was allowed to enter the promised land with Caleb; they were the only two Israelites of the original community given that privilege.

We can walk confidently in our stepparenting role by claiming the same promise Joshua clung to—the Lord goes before us and will never leave us nor forsake us. We don't have to live in fear or discouragement; the Lord walks with us. He will carry us through our stepfamily challenges until we reach the promised land that flows with milk and honey.

Too often, we try to do it alone. Our self-sufficiency gets in the way. We fail to claim God's promises and don't rely on His help. Like the Israelites wandering in the wilderness trying to find the promised land, we grumble. We think our way is best. Frustration and hopelessness follow.

Praying God's promises provides the strength and courage we need to keep going when we want to quit on our blended family journey. What promise will you claim today?

Thank You for Your promise, Lord, that You go before me. You will never leave me nor forsake me. I ask for Your help to walk confidently in my role as a stepparent.

THOUGHT FOR THE DAY

When we claim God's promises, we gain strength, courage, and comfort in our time of need.

98

More Than Conquerors

The mind governed by the flesh is death,
but the mind governed by
the Spirit is life and peace.

ROMANS 8:6

"I'm easily annoyed with the bickering between my daughter and my stepson," said Sheri. "I blew up at them again after dinner last night when they argued over whose turn it was to wash the dishes. I know I need to respond like an adult, but I can't seem to control my temper with them."

Our emotions are on overdrive in the early years as a blended family while we learn to live with different people in our home. New schedules, excessive demands on our time, and unpleasant attitudes that show up unexpectedly contribute to our feelings. But we're not the only ones going through adjustments. Our children and stepchildren also experience fragile emotions as they sort through back-and-forth routines, different rules, and new personalities.

We live in a sin-filled world full of brokenness and pain. When we allow pride and intolerance to drive our behavior, relationships break down. Healing rarely occurs if we try to cope without the help God offers.

We find answers for our hard-to-control temper and fragile emotions in Romans 8. One of the most beautiful chapters of the Bible, it describes a life lived through the Holy Spirit. It begins with "Therefore, there is now no condemnation for those who are in Christ Jesus." We're offered compassion, freedom, and forgiveness to walk in victory. We no longer have to be controlled by our flesh; we can walk confidently with a mind controlled by the Spirit.

Too often, we try to control our tempers and our tongues through willpower. Self-reliance says, "If I set my mind to it, I can stop sinning." But we need more than willpower or positive thoughts. We need God's help. We need Spirit-dependent effort to control our sinful nature.

Romans 8 comes to a beautiful conclusion: "In all these things we are more than conquerors through Him who loved us ... Neither height nor depth, nor anything else in all creation, will be able to separate us from the love of God that is in Christ Jesus our Lord."

We don't have to be slaves to our emotions. But we need the Spirit's help when our sinful nature shows up. Only then can we put aside our selfish ways that hinder relationship-building. Only then can we be "more than conquerors through Him who loved us."

Heavenly Father, I want to be a conqueror.
Help me to recognize sin's danger, turn from
self-reliance, and walk in step with Your Spirit.

THOUGHT FOR THE DAY

Life through the Spirit offers victorious living.

99

Special Days

But I will sing of your strength, in the morning I will sing of your love; for you are my fortress, my refuge in times of trouble.

PSALM 59:16

"I hate Mother's Day," the stepmom of four said as she looked at her May calendar with a somber expression. "I rarely hear from my stepchildren on that day. I don't have kids of my own, and my husband doesn't know what to do for me. Can I just ignore the day and head to the beach? No matter what I do, I feel sad and lost."

I reached over to give Karen a hug. I wanted to take her hurt away, but that wasn't possible. The truth is, special days don't always go as we'd like, for step and biological parents both. We set ourselves up with expectations that don't play out, and then we take it personally. I've done it myself, so I began to share with Karen what I'd learned.

After celebrating Mother's Day for 34 years, I now consider the expectations I carry into the holiday, especially as a stepmom. I understand my stepchildren have their own confusing emotions to deal with. Perhaps they feel it dishonors their mom to celebrate their stepmom on this special day. That's okay. I've released them of any expectations.

I believe a spouse has a role to play, however, if we're a stepparent to their kids. Be willing to give them a gentle nudge and ask for what you need. After a few less-than-stellar Mother's Days in our early years, I garnered my courage and sat my husband down for a talk. I wanted him to consider ways to acknowledge my efforts and show appreciation to me as a stepmom on Mother's Day. He was happy to oblige. Our partner's praise and honor for our role with their kids speaks volumes to us.

Years into our marriage now, I'm thankful to hear from my stepchildren on Mother's Day. But regardless of their actions, I remind myself that I serve a God who is my source of hope. He will fill me with joy and peace as I trust in Him (Romans 15:13). I affirm my worth as a stepmom and remind myself of the privilege I've been given to impact my stepchildren in a way no one else can.

Special days come and go each year, and some years have better days than others. But we can be assured that God sees us and will bless our efforts as we're mindful of our expectations, taking the high road to build healthy stepfamily relationships.

Heavenly Father, comfort me when special days leave me feeling hurt and lonely. Be my source of hope. I need You today and every day.

THOUGHT FOR THE DAY

God is my source of hope when I feel sad.

100

God's Redeeming Power

*He provided redemption for his people; he ordained his
covenant forever—holy and awesome is his name.*

PSALM 111:9

Super Bowl LII revealed an inspiring example of a team that beat the odds. The face-off happened in Minneapolis with an underdog squad, the Philadelphia Eagles, and a long-standing legend, the New England Patriots. The Eagles had overcome hardship to even make it to the playoffs. They were fighters, but no one believed they could beat the coach/quarterback duo of Bill Belichick and Tom Brady. The notorious quarterback came into the game holding impressive records and six previous Super Bowl wins. But it wasn't enough. In a suspenseful game, Philadelphia won 41–33.

It's not the win that's so impressive, though. It was how the Eagles coach Doug Pederson and backup quarterback Nick Foles responded to it. In separate postgame interviews with national coverage, both men gave credit to Jesus. Without hesitation, they acknowledged the Lord's help to overcome the odds stacked against them.

What a beautiful testimony! They didn't let culture define them. They didn't succumb to the weight of the underdog title. They knew the Lord was on their side.

We're called to do the same. With the Lord's help, we can push past the challenges and beat the odds we face in our stepfamily relationships, much like my stepmom friend Victoria has done.

Victoria calls herself a backup mom—not the title most stepmoms desire. However, she has good reason. She says, "I walked into my role with the wrong expectations. I wanted to be 'front and center' as a stepmom. I insisted on being listed on school emergency forms and involved in every aspect of my stepchildren's lives. It eventually backfired, though. Their mom resented me and turned her kids against me. I learned the hard way that I'm not their main mom. I'm there to help when my stepchildren need me—and I'm readily available—but they have a mom capable of taking care of them." Like a backup quarterback, she now steps in only when asked.

I asked Victoria how she changed her position. "God clearly spoke to me one day as I studied the book of Romans," she said. "It hit me like a firecracker bang when I read, 'Honor one another above yourselves' (Romans 12:10). I knew I wasn't honoring my stepkids' mom. I was creating dissension by expecting a certain place in my stepchildren's lives. I sensed God telling me to view my role differently; to step back and honor their mom's position in their lives. As a result, our relationships have taken ten steps forward."

Are you facing unfavorable circumstances? With the Lord's redemptive help, you can work through the differences in your stepfamily relationships. Don't give up. You can beat the odds!

We need Your redeeming power in our stepfamily, Lord.
Help us forge ahead through our challenges
and move to smoother waters.

> ### THOUGHT FOR THE DAY
>
> With God's help, we can work through our differences
> and beat the odds in stepfamily relationships.

101

The Power of Surrender

If only you would prepare your heart and lift up your hands to him in prayer!
JOB 11:13 NLT

The idea of surrender can be uncomfortable. For some, it feels weak or submissive. What does it really mean? The definition says, "to give oneself up, as into the power of another; to submit or yield." Surrender means we relinquish control and stop insisting things go our way.

Stepfamily life is messy. We seldom find easy answers to our challenges. Just this morning, I received a text from a stepmom who said, "I'm about at the end of my rope." My heart aches for her. I understand the struggle.

I've worked with blended families from all over the United States and Canada, and even one stepmom from the country of Norway. Although the specifics in each home are different, many of the issues are the same. The dynamics are complicated. The challenges are many. The road is bumpy.

How do we find peace and contentment when we trudge down a dark road? Where do we go for help with our hard emotions? One word gives us the answer: *surrender*.

- Surrender to a loving God who's working in your life for good; don't always question His ways.
- Surrender to the tension of budding relationships; give love time to grow.
- Surrender to your circumstances in their present state; don't wish for something different.
- Surrender to your feelings of loss; ask for God's help to overcome your grief.
- Surrender to the disharmony in your home; don't ask others to make changes they're not capable of yet.

- Surrender to a need for God's help; start every day with prayer.
- Surrender to imperfect love; find contentment in progress.
- Surrender to change and an unknown future; trust God who never changes.
- Surrender to the release of control; accept that things can be okay even when they don't go your way.
- Surrender to uncomfortable conversations; open your mind to new and purposeful thinking.
- Surrender to a marriage between two imperfect people; commit to do your part to create lasting love.
- Surrender your heart to an omnipotent God who loves you. Surrender your trust to His sovereignty. Surrender your circumstances to His plan. Surrender your will to His.

I surrender all. All to You, Lord Jesus, I surrender all.

THOUGHT FOR THE DAY

We find peace on our journey when we surrender.

God's Redeeming Power: Reflect on It

1. God's promises provide comfort, strength, and courage. What is your favorite promise? Here's one I turn to often: "Do not fear, for I am with you; do not be dismayed, for I am your God. I will strengthen you and help you; I will uphold you with my righteous right hand" (Isaiah 41:10).

2. What challenge do you need God's help with? Take time to reread "The Promise of God's Power" and ask for His help with expectant hope.

3. Would you rather have a different set of circumstances in your blended family? Consider the story of Elisabeth Elliot and her powerful message: "The secret is Christ in me."

4. What source do you first turn to for answers? A friend, a book, the internet, prayer? Meditate on 1 Corinthians 1:25.

5. Surrender can bring peace to an anxious heart. Do you need to surrender your trust to His sovereignty? Surrender your circumstances to His plan? Surrender your will to His will? I encourage you, today and every day, to surrender to a loving God who's working in your life for good.

Acknowledgments

I'm indebted to a group of family, friends, and work associates who provided ongoing support and encouragement to make this book possible. Writing is a solitary task, but the outpouring of love and support along the way offers an auxiliary weapon needed to complete the mission.

First, my dear husband, Randy. Although our family of seven could have used a steadier income when our kids were young and I honed my craft as a writer, you continued to support my efforts and encourage my publishing dreams. Thank you for believing in me, Randy.

My sister and fellow stepmom, Jan Gull, has been my biggest cheerleader through every step. Thank you, Jan, for your encouragement to follow my heart to help blended families and for your inspiring words on hard days to push through until I completed the task.

My beloved mom went to be with Jesus many years ago, but her words of affirmation continue to float in my mind. My dad—an author himself—empowered me to pursue my publishing goals, despite the obstacles. Thank you for the reminder, Dad, that "Most books never get published because they don't get written."

Thank you to my prayer warrior, Andrea Lazenby, who diligently prayed with me through every phase of the project, reminding me of God's power and faithfulness to the end.

I'm thankful for my writers' critique group who encouraged my publishing efforts and helped me develop my craft. A big thank you to the leader of the group, Sandi Tompkins, who provided a loving nudge toward disciplined writing and the pursuit of excellence. I appreciate your continued guidance and mentorship of my writing projects, Sandi.

I appreciate the efforts of my hardworking agent, Karen Neumair of Credo Communications, who has walked alongside me for almost a decade and continues to provide invaluable advice with my publishing needs. Thank you, Karen, for your wise and kind counsel.

A special thank you to Vice President of Publishing Rob Teigen and Christian Art Gifts. Thank you, Rob, for your willingness to support blended families and their needs.

Thank you, stepparents and coaching clients, who poured out your hearts and relayed your stories in search of answers. I pray this devotional provides the encouragement you need to keep going on days you want to quit, empowering words to help you thrive in your blended family relationships, and a renewed desire to seek God's grace and guidance for your road.

About Gayla Grace

Gayla Grace is a wife to Randy, mom and stepmom to five adult children, Adrianne, Payton, Jamie, Jodi, and Nathan, mother-in-law to Torin, Jacob, Jamie, and Trisella, and a proud grandma to Harvest and Millie. She and her husband, Randy, have been married for almost three decades with a "his, hers, and ours" family and are now enjoying their empty nest season with travel, hiking, and good cups of coffee on their front porch together.

Their early years of marriage brought unexpected challenges, and blending their children didn't come easily. In time, however, they learned how to parent together and form a united team.

Because of the bumpy road they have traveled, Gayla is passionate about helping other blended families create harmony in their relationships and work through common dynamics such as loyalty conflicts, birth order changes, rebellious stepchildren, holiday strife, competing schedules, financial struggles, and difficult ex-spouses.

Gayla serves on staff with FamilyLife Blended, a division of FamilyLife, as a writer and a speaker. She ministers to blended families through national events, podcasts, live streams, and other media.

She has a master's degree in psychology and counseling and has been helping stepfamilies for more than two decades. She is the coauthor of a stepmom devotional, *Quiet Moments for the Stepmom Soul*, and a holiday e-book, *Unwrapping the Gift of Stepfamily Peace*, both of which are available on Amazon.

In addition, Gayla was the cofounder and director of Sisterhood of Stepmoms for many years, a nonprofit organization designed to create community and provide national retreats for stepmothers.

Find out more about Gayla Grace at gaylagrace.com.

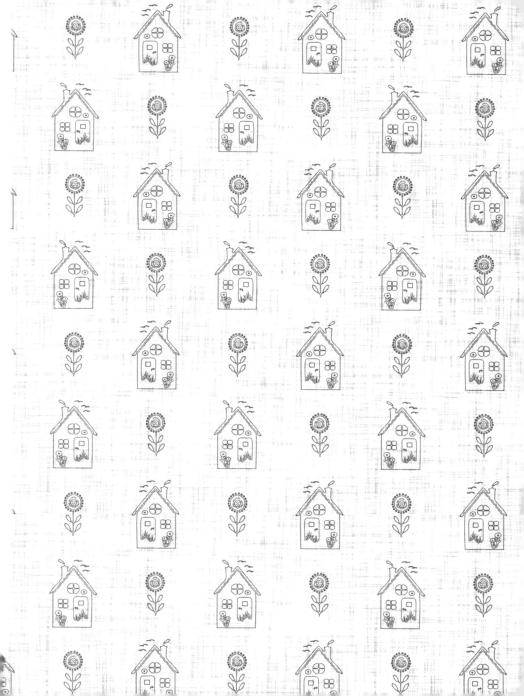